THE RIGHT TO BE FORGOTTEN

RISJ CHALLENGES

CHALLENGES present findings, analysis, and recommendations from Oxford's Reuters Institute for the Study of Journalism. The Institute is dedicated to the rigorous, international comparative study of journalism, in all its forms and on all continents. CHALLENGES muster evidence and research to take forward an important argument, beyond the mere expression of opinions. Each text is carefully reviewed by an editorial committee, drawing where necessary on the advice of leading experts in the relevant fields. CHALLENGES remain, however, the work of authors writing in their individual capacities, not a collective expression of views from the Institute.

EDITORIAL COMMITTEE

Timothy Garton Ash
Ian Hargreaves
David Levy
Geert Linnebank
John Lloyd
Rasmus Kleis Nielsen
James Painter
Alan Rusbridger
Jean Seaton
Katrin Voltmer

The Reuters Institute would like to acknowledge the assistance of Peggy Valcke and Timothy Garton Ash as editorial advisers on behalf of the Institute.

THE RIGHT TO BE FORGOTTEN

PRIVACY AND THE MEDIA IN THE DIGITAL AGE

GEORGE BROCK

Published by I.B.Tauris & Co. Ltd in association with
the Reuters Institute for the Study of Journalism, University of Oxford

Published in 2016 by
I.B.Tauris & Co. Ltd
London • New York
www.ibtauris.com

Copyright © 2016 George Brock

The right of George Brock to be identified as the author of this work has been asserted by the author in accordance with the Copyright, Designs and Patents Act 1988.

All rights reserved. Except for brief quotations in a review, this book, or any part thereof, may not be reproduced, stored in or introduced into a retrieval system, or transmitted, in any form or by any means, electronic, mechanical, photocopying, recording or otherwise, without the prior written permission of the publisher.

References to websites were correct at the time of writing.

ISBN: 978 1 78453 592 6
eISBN: 978 1 78672 112 9
ePDF: 978 1 78673 112 8

A full CIP record for this book is available from the British Library
A full CIP record is available from the Library of Congress

Library of Congress Catalog Card Number: available

Typeset by Riverside Publishing Solutions, Salisbury, SP4 6NQ
Printed and bound in Great Britain by T.J. International, Padstow, Cornwall

Contents

About the Author — vi

Acknowledgements — vii

1. Law, Power, and the Hyperlink — 1
2. The Search Society — 17
3. Striking the Balance — 31
4. Google Spain — 38
5. Reactions and Consequences — 45
6. Beyond Europe — 63
7. New Law: The General Data Protection Regulation — 73
8. Alternative Approaches — 82
9. Conclusions: The Future — 89

Notes — 102

Bibliography — 111

Index — 113

About the Author

George Brock is Professor of Journalism at City, University of London, where he directed studies in journalism 2009–14. He is co-leader of a research team at the university investigating search tools for journalism which has received grants from Google in 2015 and 2016 under the company's computational journalism and digital news initiatives. He has worked for the *Observer* and *The Times*. At *The Times* he was Foreign Editor and Managing Editor; he was the paper's correspondent in Brussels, 1991–5. He has been on the board of the World Editors Forum and the International Press Institute. In 2013 he published *Out of Print: Newspapers, Journalism and the Business of News in the Digital Age*.

Acknowledgements

I am grateful first and foremost to David Levy of the Reuters Institute for encouraging this study and to his colleagues Rasmus Kleis Nielsen and Alex Reid for their scrupulous editorial care and attention. I would also like to thank Peggy Valcke, Timothy Garton Ash, Daniel Wilsher, Judith Townend, and Martin Moore for their helpful comments. None bear any responsibility for faults. My greatest debt, as always, is to my wife Kay.

1

Law, Power, and the Hyperlink

Until recently, the English phrase a 'right to be forgotten' suggested fiction rather than reality. Fans of the *Men In Black* films think immediately of the 'neuralyser', the pen-shaped device which, when pointed at someone's head and activated, wipes out memory. Or it might bring to mind Winston Smith, the protagonist of George Orwell's *1984*, whose dreary job as a censor of history involves removing articles no longer thought politically acceptable from back copies of *The Times*.

In May 2014, arguments erupted over the 'right to be forgotten' in real life. The phrase had been written and spoken before then, but very largely in the specialised world of 'data protection'. The controversy began with a landmark judgment by the European Court of Justice, the highest court in the European Union.

The court decided that the vast, US-based search engine Google was subject to EU data protection law, that it had responsibilities under that law, and that it was required to remove search links when requests from citizens to do so met certain tests. The third of these decisions came instantly to be known as 'the right to be forgotten'. The name is variously used to cover both the de-indexing (or delisting) of internet search results and the deletion of digital material. The phrase is neither new nor, when applied to de-indexing, wholly accurate. But as a slogan it was an instant and resounding success. That success owed a lot to accumulated anxieties about the potential harm which can be caused by some information stored and searchable on the internet.

The judgment in the case formally known as *C-131/12 Google Spain SL and Google Inc v. AEPD and Mario Costeja Gonzalez* (and usually known as 'Google Spain') was a shock.[1] Google had expected to win the case. Advice to the court from its Advocate-General had recommended that the balance between freedom of speech and privacy should be struck by refusing the request to take the information out of Google's search index. The court's decision came as a surprise for another reason: very few people knew much about data protection law and especially about this aspect of it.

The 'right to be forgotten' is only one part of data protection but its workings deserve to be much better known and debated. The question of whether the law should require personal information to be delisted by search engines (or deleted altogether) sits at the new, shifting, and disputed border between free speech and privacy in the online world. Battles over privacy have now become struggles over digital information rights. A new dispensation between freedom of information and rights to protect privacy and reputation is being hammered out in courts and political systems across the world. The search for a way to manage this collision of rights did not start with the Google Spain case, but that judgment tilted, polarised and fired up the debate.

Digital technology, by making possible vastly greater creation, storage, and search of information, poses new questions about free speech, privacy, and rights of rectification. Timeless values need to be applied in new contexts. This study examines the origins of, and fallout from, Google Spain and questions whether the balance is being struck in the right place. Any intervention at the junction of journalism, law, and technology should be closely examined and monitored. Journalism also plays a role in public memory. Exactly how much do we want to be able to recall? How do we determine what that is?

Free speech and privacy have been colliding for centuries. Rights which clash often cannot be reconciled; they can only be balanced by reasoning from the facts of a case. The debate over the 'right to be forgotten' opens a window on our attempts to adapt long-established values and principles to the online world. It poses questions for law and democracy raised by globalisation and instant communication. The issue is not only the competition of free speech and privacy but of discovery, historical memory, forgetting, the integrity of the public record, the right to know, and forgiveness. We are gradually assembling the conventions, software code and laws of a new public sphere.

The basic questions asked in the Google Spain case were: can Google's search algorithm cause harm? If so, what should be done? Much of the immediate reaction to the case was overblown: it was not legal authority for the neuralyser or real-life Winston Smiths. The fact that people overreacted to the judgment does not mean that the European Court issued a good decision, nor does it mean that there are no future risks to free speech built into it. The decision in Google Spain will come, I would argue, to be seen as one of the poorest in the court's history. It makes the best balance between both freedom of speech and of knowledge – fundamental to good journalism – and the protection of privacy harder to achieve.

The judgment stores up trouble for the future by leaving important questions unresolved. A central one, still in dispute at the time of writing, turns on the territorial scope and enforceability of legal rulings about the internet, which by its nature recognises no borders. Regulatory jurisdiction and the transnational flow of information are mismatched. The judges said nothing about how far the right to be forgotten should reach. Google interpreted the ruling as applying to Europe: links removed were at first visible to those searching on the relevant names from an EU domain (google.co.uk, google.de, google.fr, etc.) but could be found by switching to google.com. European data protection authorities said that restricting the judgment's effect to Europe would make it too easy to evade. The French authority[2] began legal action against Google. The company attempted to defuse the stand-off by limiting the workaround. But the French authority insists that anything less than worldwide effect frustrates enforcement of the court's wish. Google argues that worldwide application harms the information rights of people who are not EU citizens.[3]

The right to be forgotten and journalism

Decisions which mark the new frontier between the right to free expression, the right to know, privacy, and data protection have significant implications for journalism. Journalism may pursue long-established aims, but the channels of communication have changed. If we define journalism as the systematic attempt to establish the truth of what matters to society in real time, that aim remains as important as ever in an information-saturated world. There are more providers and sources of information; that multiplies opportunities to learn but it also provides new opportunities to deceive. I have argued elsewhere[4] that journalism in the twenty-first century faces four 'core' tasks: verification, sense-making, eye-witness, and investigation (of wrongdoing or dishonesty). Free expression rights underpin journalism and are pivotal in an additional sense. Journalism sometimes operates at the edge of what is permitted, tolerated, or legal in order to disclose unexpected, concealed, or unwanted facts. This is true outside totalitarian or authoritarian states in which the law's boundaries are often journalists' main preoccupations.

Those tasks face new challenges in a world of newly malleable information. In the words of a Dutch court giving judgment in a case about the 'right to be forgotten', the internet is 'an ocean of information' which can change at any moment.[5] Previous ideas of free speech underpinning journalism rested on the assumption that a fixed (printed) record should not be suppressed or interfered with. The quantity of recorded information and the ability instantly to change it suggest that long-standing principles must be rethought and applied in different ways. This study outlines one part of that rethinking.

Journalism must also navigate new distribution routes. Access to the consumers of news is now increasingly by search engines and social networks, predominantly Google and Facebook. As one study of this new information power puts it:

> *Almost accidentally, these global tech giants have taken on civic roles, and with these roles, civic power. This includes the power to enable collective action, the power to communicate news, and the power to influence people's vote.*[6]

From the seventeenth to twentieth centuries, journalism's move to be independent (above all of the power of the state) altered the governance of democracies. New communications technologies raise the same issues of making power accountable, but in new form in the twenty-first century. Journalists have celebrated the freedoms, diversity, and new opportunities that digital distribution offers but are now looking at the consequences of a major shift in control. This new power also needs to be accountable. To hold power to account, journalism depends on the understanding that neither individuals nor organisations have an unqualified right to control information about themselves. The issue at the heart of the right to be forgotten is how much control should be given to individuals to deal with the unforeseen effects of new technologies.

In the words of James Ball of Buzzfeed (writing in the *Guardian*):

> *Whether you are an ardent First Amendment advocate or a passionate believer that networks must do more to police their backyards, the worst of all possible worlds for the flow of information is one in which we shift*

from the rule of democratic law to one governed by the arbitrary, inconsistent and perhaps kneejerk rulings of a tiny group of large companies.[7]

Digital downside

Most new means of communication, from air travel to the internet, are greeted with uncritical enthusiasm. As risks and disadvantages become more obvious after the initial promise, anxieties emerge. The cheap processors, sensors, and networks which drive digital information at such speed and volume have radically lowered the cost of access to that information. Digital communications are both an engine of opportunity and an unprecedented opportunity for surveillance. New public policies can be tried, new businesses are born, new means of accountability are available. An unprecedented scale of commercial ambition is possible: companies like Google and Facebook aim to persuade the whole population of the planet to become their customers.

These technologies have put publishing power in the hands of a few billion people. We have discovered that they are empowering and disempowering at the same time. Digital devices knit together our private, social, and working lives. Our ability to capture, store, and distribute information has multiplied the amount of information in existence by huge orders of magnitude. One leading estimate of the world's data reckons that its total quantity doubles every two years. By this count, the world held 4.4 zettabytes in 2013 and will hold 44 zettabytes by 2020.[8] The more data the world gathers, the further the opportunities extend for comparison and data crunching. Some of this analysis is innovative and useful, but it has a downside. Companies which 'scrape' the web dig up old police mugshots and display them online in the hope that people will pay to take them down. There are 16 sensors in the average smartphone. From the data they report, journalism could be adjusted and produced in response to the location, mood, and activity of the phone user. But that data could also rate the user's sociability or attractiveness to other people. Phones are only the most prominent devices which accumulate data about everyone who uses them. Credit cards and cars do the same.

Stockpiles of data alter our ideas of how we record the life of a society and how the public space functions. Speaking of newspapers, people used the phrase 'paper of record' to describe a reliably accurate one. This idea could only take shape in a society with a limited amount of public information which could be thought of as a 'record'. Major national libraries attempt to capture at regular intervals everything that is on the internet. Is that now the historical record? Even if captured, digital information is malleable, correctable, and can be changed quickly. The abundance of information forces us to think more carefully about what we try to record and what we might reasonably lose, forget, or obscure. The internet offers unprecedented opportunities for voyeurism, exhibitionism, and morning-after regret. The internet is not a library: much of it is not edited in any way, much of it is not aimed at public purpose of any kind, websites are more perishable than books and access to it is given by private companies which are occasionally revealed to be manipulating results for commercial ends.

But the sheer range of information now accessible – and even its random and anarchic, unorganised nature – is part of what many people celebrate about the internet. Search engines and social networks increase the diversity of the news people consume.[9] Journalists no longer have a monopoly on the production of information which has public value – if they ever did. To protect and preserve information of public value we need to consider carefully the contours and boundaries not only of what helps the public interest now but of what might in the future.

Uncontrolled heterogeneous documents

In their original academic paper which laid out the problems of searching the World Wide Web and how they proposed to solve them, the founders of Google, Sergey Brin and Larry Page, wrote: 'The web is a vast collection of completely uncontrolled heterogeneous documents'.[10] Here are three recent examples of the fragments of information which different people wanted removed from the vast collection in public circulation or made harder to find.

- In 2009 lawyers for an ex-convict in Germany, Wolfgang Werlé, attempted to remove his name from the English version of Wikipedia. Werlé, with Manfred Lauber, had been convicted in 1993 of the murder of a prominent German actor, Walter Sedlmayr, in a trial which received wide coverage. Werlé's lawyers cited German privacy law precedents which allow the erasure of a criminal's name once he or she has served the sentence. Wikipedia and its parent, the Wikimedia Foundation, refused the request and successfully defended that decision in US courts. German courts made judgments in favour of the convicted men but the Constitutional Court overruled these as unreasonable restrictions on free speech. On the German-language Wikipedia.de there is no article on either man, while a search in the same site for 'Walter Sedlmayr' still carries the names of his killers. The English-language versions were untouched. The editing of the German site was voluntarily done by Wikipedia's editors in Germany. The Wikimedia Foundation says that this is down to the respective Wikipedia language 'communities'. 'We support both user communities in these decisions', the Foundation says.[11]

- In 2006, horrible pictures of a young woman who had been decapitated in a car crash in California began circulating on the internet. The pictures had been routinely taken at the scene by Highway Patrol staff who had later posted them on the web for friends at Halloween. American privacy laws do not cover such a case and First Amendment freedoms limit the ability to take down internet material. A recently founded company, Reputation.com, helped to get the pictures off more than 2,000 websites. But, to the continuing distress of the victim's family, they could still be found years later.[12]

- In December 2015, a court in Saitama, Japan, ordered Google to remove from their search index reports of the arrest and fine of a man for violating child prostitution and pornography laws. The presiding judge said that convicted criminals were entitled to have their private life respected and their 'rehabilitation unhindered'. Google is appealing the decision.[13]

These cases are all reactions to changes in information power over the past two decades: what information can do and who controls that. Public unease has prompted the makers of law and policy to question the ideas which have governed communications until the digital age. Artemi Rallo Lombarte, a Spanish MP and once head of Spain's data protection agency:

> *The right to be forgotten does conflict with freedom of expression. Internet users are not entitled to access personal information on the internet. We have to adapt our ideas of what free expression allows.*[14]

By the end of 2014, there were seven billion mobile phones on the planet, roughly equal to the earth's population. By 2017, one-third of those will probably be smartphones.[15] We are taking something like a trillion pictures a year on our phones, a number which has doubled in the past five years. In the course of each minute, 200 million people send email messages, YouTube users upload 72 hours of video, and Facebook users exchange 2.5 million pieces of content. Each minute of each day.[16] More than 90 per cent of internet searches in Europe are on Google; its share of mobile search is 96 per cent. A global survey of platforms which capture, transmit, and process data to create giant networks found 64 in the US, 82 in Asia, and 27 in Europe. The aggregate market cap of the American companies in that 2015 survey was $3,123bn. The equivalent figure for Europe $181bn.[17] Some of that valuation lay in a new class of asset: data. Much of that can be classified as 'personal'.

The scale of these corporations provokes suspicion, envy, and opposition. Blogs and pundits in France refer to 'GAFA', standing for Google, Apple, Facebook, and Amazon – all tech giants, all American. Others call those companies 'Prism' corporations, a sarcastic reference to the one of the US government's most notorious and once-secret surveillance programmes, mounted with help from some parts of Silicon Valley. The informatics scholar Shoshana Zuboff describes Google's ambitions as 'surveillance capitalism':

> The game is no longer about sending you a mail order catalog or even about targeting online advertising. The game is selling access to the real-time flow of your daily life – your reality – in order to directly influence and modify your behavior for profit.
>
> … We've entered virgin territory here. The assault on behavioral data is so sweeping that it can no longer be circumscribed by the concept of privacy and its contests. … In the fullness of time, we will look back on the establishment in Europe of the 'Right to be Forgotten' and the EU's more recent invalidation of the Safe Harbor doctrine[18] as early milestones in a gradual reckoning with the true dimensions of this challenge.[19]

The excitement with which people adopted search engines and social networks reflected a need which they met. That initial enthusiasm has now worn off and been mixed with suspicion and resentment. Both moods reflect shifts of informational power. The first shift was in favour of consumers and users who could enjoy a range of instant information never before available. The second shift has been a slowly accumulating resistance to the power of the new gatekeepers who so influence daily life.

Opportunities to capture and distribute information were dispersed by digital devices. But the ability to accumulate, store, search, and analyse expanded the power of the data harvesters by unforeseen magnitudes. The power of instant retrieval alters the normal effects of the passage of time: information need not fade into the past but can be returned to the present with a keystroke.

> *Whether an ill-advised remark was made this morning or 20 years ago, if it comes up in an online search it is still, in some important sense, part of the here and now. Only with the greatest difficulty can stuff be entirely removed, the published unpublished.*[20]

The idea that information, more and more of it, is simply liberating has given way to a more nuanced picture. Governments have barely begun to work out how to handle the power of the new superpowers of cyberspace. Policymakers have hardly grappled with the questions of how to treat internet intermediaries such as Google and Facebook. The public is the creator of most new data and both the beneficiary and, sometimes, victim of its retention, processing, and deployment. In twenty-first-century life 'to exist is to be indexed by a search engine'.[21]

Facebook has over 35 million users in the UK. Ofcom's survey for 2014 reported that 65 per cent of its users in the UK claimed to have tightened their privacy settings. A YouGov survey reported that Facebook lost 9 per cent of its UK users in the year to the middle of 2014. Half of those who stopped cited targeted advertising or other privacy concerns. 'In the internet, humans have created an infinite new continent', Caitlin Moran, a columnist for *The Times* wrote, 'A limitless, seething megalopolis in which we do everything in a real megalopolis – shop, chat, meet – but in which we seem to believe the laws that humans painstakingly constructed ... don't count.' Moran concluded that column: 'But nothing is free, and everything a human ever does counts.'[22]

Public opinion is ambivalent and shifting. In a Eurobarometer survey of 2011, 73 per cent of respondents from throughout the EU said that they would like to give their specific approval before the collection and processing of their personal information. But it must be likely that a large number of those have technically given their approval by clicking 'yes' on privacy conditions or cookie access requests without, in most cases, having much idea of exactly what they've agreed to. Three-quarters of Europeans polled wanted to be able to delete personal information on a website whenever they decided to do so. Sixty-three per cent said that disclosing personal information was a 'big issue' for them. Exactly the same percentage had not heard of any public authority responsible for the protection of rights on personal data.[23] Research from 2012 by Consumer Futures found that one in ten consumers had not realised any data was collected on them via online services, and a further fifth thought that the provider only collected the minimum amount required to make the service work better. Privacy, Facebook's founder Mark Zuckerberg once said, is no longer the 'social norm' that it once was.[24]

Attitudes and knowledge vary considerably between EU countries. A 2014 survey found that 1 per cent of respondents in the UK had heard of the national data protection authority, the Information Commissioner's Office. The figure for France was almost 70 per cent, up from 50 per cent only two years before. There is nothing particularly surprising in these variations. Policies and laws which manage a shifting reconciliation between free speech and privacy are usually the product of long, delicate compromise-making inside a single political culture.

Reputation and remembering

One purpose of this study is to point the way to how wired societies might best deal with digital platforms which are new sources of influence and power, often not 'publishers' in the classic sense, but making decisions which shape, edit, colour, and rank what people can find. The creation and distribution of information, news, and opinion has always been subject to some constraints imposed by society. Strong allegiance to the value and ideas of free speech does not prevent societies – America included – from occasionally restraining self-expression. Simply to equate freedom of speech with lack of regulation is to dodge the difficult issue of how such laws and rules can be as limited as possible and work as precisely and effectively as possible.

Professor Viktor Mayer-Schönberger of Oxford thinks that we should worry less about remembering than about forgetting – something human societies were good at before the internet. He sees the accumulation, search, and retrieval of the twenty-first century as the culmination of a long historical process by which human societies have become steadily more exact and retentive about information. European societies archived little until the eighteenth century; the nineteenth century brought name registers, listed place names, collective memory with mass media. In the second half of the twentieth century, people began to worry about the misuse of data, but protection of data rarely kept up with the advances of technology. Now, he says, we need pragmatic ways to remember less. We do not need to delete things but to think about how easy or hard it is to reach them. 'Until now, we have mostly worried about how things are recorded,' he says, 'now, we have to think about how they are retrieved. That is because the default has shifted from forgetting to remembering.'[25]

In law, one of those efforts has been 'data protection'. Laws about data protection long predate the accelerating anxieties about social media and privacy in the early years of the new millennium. The Google Spain judgment of 2014 was based on an EU directive of 1995 which, not surprisingly, makes no mention of the internet.[26] The directive, whose scope is sweeping, generated laws which altered many business practices but it also established a tradition of such law declaring grand and noble aims which were then ignored and bypassed by proliferating digital innovations. Internet researcher Joris van Hoboken, who advised the European Commission on new data protection law, noticed this gap between theory and practice:

> The web is full of legal issues. And that's a direct consequence of the fact that people can publish things themselves without having the information checked by an editorial office. Quite a bit of what's published on social media, and especially pictures, is just plainly illegal in Europe. Small and large violations of privacy are commonplace.[27]

The key ideas which formed that 1995 directive (a template for laws in each EU state) have long antecedents and are strongly held by a majority of governments. People worry about the misuse of data but share personal information energetically. Many of the ideas from the first directive are reproduced in the new regulation on data protection, due to enter force in 2018.[28] The regulation will bind governments more tightly than a directive and it aims to reduce inconsistencies in enforcement between states.

The protection of honour

The protection of personal data from unauthorised misuse has its roots in strong legal traditions – especially in France, Germany, Spain, and Italy – which allow individuals to control their reputation, image, and 'honour' (the best equivalent in English of a term for which there is no exact translation).[29] Those ideas are also popular in Central Europe. Germany remembers the information control of both the Nazi regime and the East German secret police, the Stasi. The drive to protect personal data has powerful momentum derived from recent memory. Thirteen European countries have put data protection in their constitutions. The head of France's data protection authority, when recommending to a parliamentary commission that rights to data protection should be included in the French constitution, stressed that the right to control personal data is now distinct from the right to protect private life.

The internet is massively accumulative, searchable in a second, and, despite the extensive decay of hyperlinks, can preserve information indefinitely. That changes the nature of debates about rectification, something legal scholars call 'practical obscurity' (referring to a piece of information not erased but hard to find), and forgetting. The internet is both retentive and imperfect. The first page of search results for any given term, perhaps ten hyperlinks, is by far the commonest source of internet information.

Put the same term into three different search engines and you will get different results. They may overlap, but they will not be identical. So algorithms written by humans make value judgements. They may process data automatically and at extraordinary speed but they have power to affect human lives by choosing what the searcher sees and sees first.

This was exactly what bothered Mario Costeja Gonzalez, a lawyer and calligraphy expert living in Barcelona. In 1998, Sr Costeja had been the subject of a court order which allowed the authorities to auction his property to recover social security debts. The auction was publicised in two unadorned 36-word announcements a week apart in Barcelona's principal daily newspaper, *La Vanguardia*. When anyone searched for 'Mario Costeja Gonzalez' on Google in 2010, the 12-year-old notice of his bankruptcy and auction of his furniture was at the top of the results.

Sr Costeja lodged a complaint with the Spanish data protection authority (the AEPD[30]) to have the announcements erased from both

Google Spain and from *La Vanguardia*'s archive. The AEPD's then director, Artemi Rallo Lombarte, took a close interest in how individuals could strengthen control of their reputation. He had long been convinced, he said, that a compromise was possible by which the record would not be taken out of the original archive but that it would be made harder to find by being removed from a search engine. One of the first complaints to come before him was from a university teacher who had been fined in the 1980s for urinating in the street. Every year, his students would Google his 25-year-old minor conviction, their clicks on the link keeping the item near the top of the search results.

So the AEPD broke new ground by ruling that Sr Costeja did have the right to ask Google to erase its links to the notices even if the original newspaper archive still held them. In the later words of the European Court,

> *The AEPD took the view that it has the power to require the withdrawal of data and the prohibition of access to certain data by the operators of search engines when it considers that the locating and dissemination of the data are liable to compromise the fundamental right to data protection and the dignity of persons in the broad sense …*[31]

The AEPD's decision went to the Spanish high court and was promptly referred to the EU judges in Luxembourg.

The claim that a search engine link breached 'the fundamental right to data protection' is crucial. Many legal systems allow restrictions on freedom of expression when a litigant claims that information circulated or published has done harm. All EU states and America have such laws. Examples would include defamation (or libel), breaches of privacy, or certain kinds of incitement. Many states forbid, under varying conditions, the republication of criminal convictions to help the rehabilitation of offenders. But data protection laws, drawn from from an EU directive, include wider powers to control personal information which do not depend on being able to show that harm has been done. Data protection law was originally conceived to give individuals rights of access and rectification concerning information held on them by states, companies, and organisations. It was not designed to regulate speech or expression.

There is further detailed discussion of the EU court's reasoning in Chapter 4. Two points stand out here. First, any debate over how to manage conflicting rights is upended in the final judgment by the sweeping and powerful phrasing of data protection as an emerging right. Second, the tests which determine whether or not information can be removed from public view are framed in words which are so vague as to multiply confusion and not to reduce it.

The new infrastructure of knowledge

Open democracies have long legislated to remove some information from circulation. Companies like Google edit their output. Before the Spanish case, Google already had in place a system for handling deletion requests: bank account and credit card numbers, images of signatures are taken down as well as around a million links a day in response to requests arising from claims of copyright breach.[32] Courts in the UK and elsewhere can order certain sorts of information – libel, breaches of confidence or privacy, the identification of children in litigation, for example – not be published.

Many European states have laws which prohibit mention of past lesser crimes when the crimes are 'spent'. Several have media conventions that people convicted of (at least some) crimes are not referred to afterwards by their full names. But these measures differ from country to country. Victims of domestic abuse, often named when their partners are on trial, want to start new lives free from association with their past. Should they be granted anonymity in court or a right to be forgotten afterwards? Who should decide? The best argument for a 'right to delisting' is empowerment – that people who are harmed or distressed by something about them on the internet and who do not have the resources to hire lawyers can fix something that is wrong.

The Google Spain case reveals a gap in thinking about the new infrastructure of knowledge. We rely completely on intermediaries like Google, Bing, and Yahoo to use the colossal archives stored online. This study could not have been written without the ability, provided largely by google.co.uk, for the author to locate hundreds of relevant items. But the law has not yet adapted to intermediaries. As Joe McNamee of the European Digital Rights Initiative summarises:

> We have a big problem in Europe with how we treat online intermediaries. Should risks of terrorism, hate speech and simple abuse or embarrassment all be handled in the same way or not? We don't seem to know. The current political approach appears to assume that the internet giants can solve all the world's problems.[33]

The Google Spain judgment provoked noisy outcry which immediately engaged the spokespersons of the 'deletionists' and the 'preservationists'. Much of the fuss died down as soon as the complexities of the law and background emerged. Data protection is intricate and a 'right not to be found by Google' is considerably less dramatic than a 'right to be forgotten'. Google complained about the decision (and discreetly encouraged other voices to do so) but the company had good reason to fulfil the court's requirement without delay. Google faces two huge anti-trust investigations by the European Commission which will last for years and either of which, if the decision goes against Google, could derail or seriously damage its business model across the EU.

Google set up a web form which allows complainants to identify links which they want taken down and to justify their complaint. Google provides only bare statistics about how many complaints it has processed. By August 2016 and over two years after the judgment, a total of 539,384 applications had been made; 1,652,417 URLs had been 'evaluated', and 43.1 per cent of the total had been de-indexed.[34] A sample of figures by country is given in the following table.

Country	Applications	URLs evaluated	Percentage de-indexed
UK	94,937	218,682	38.9
France	133,066	337,634	49.0
Germany	80,598	291,865	48.3
Spain	46,029	140,465	38.3
Italy	37,780	115,910	32.3
Poland	12,623	48,447	42.2
Sweden	12,260	45,935	41.8
Netherlands	27,104	94,748	45.7

Google has resisted all calls to provide a deeper or more detailed analysis of how it decides these cases, although its executives have given broad and general descriptions of the tests they use. A number of UK news publishers, including the BBC, either kept a public list of links taken down or republished stories which they thought should have stayed in the record. As Google's force of paralegals fielded hundreds of thousand requests, a relatively small proportion led to adjudications by national data protection authorities or to court cases.[35] The only leak of detailed data suggests that the large majority of requests are not about news or directed at news sites.[36]

Evaluating risks to freedom of speech or privacy is not a question of quantity. For the time being the system which has been tacked together on the back of existing data protection law seems to have worked quite well. But does it nevertheless represent a risk of harm – either to freedom of speech or to privacy, or to both – in the longer term? Data protection began with the understandable and laudable aim of protecting individuals from the misuse of state and corporate information. But does the pursuit of those aims in practice satisfy the public interest? The answer to that requires a look at the intellectual roots of data protection.

2

The Search Society

There is no internationally recognised and enforceable basic 'right' to be forgotten. The European Convention on Human Rights guarantees the right to privacy (Article 8) and the right to free expression (Article 10). The UN Declaration of Human Rights covers the same ground in Articles 12 and 19. The EU Charter of Fundamental Rights[1] guarantees the right to privacy (Article 7), the right to data protection (Article 8), and the right to free expression (Article 11). The UK's Human Rights Act reiterates the rights in the European Convention. None of these documents talk of a right to be delisted, forgotten, or erased.

In part this reflects history: these are rights written in the pre-digital age. The UK's Human Rights Act, the most recent of the codes listed above, was passed in 1998 when the internet was a few years old and in the year that Google was first incorporated as a company. But the EU's Charter does include a right to data protection in Article 8. The EU's new regulation on data protection does include a section under the title 'Right to erasure ("right to be forgotten")'.[2]

Support for entirely unregulated freedom of speech on the internet has shrunk as the costs of the free flows of information have become more evident. Cass Sunstein argued that its very openness carried risks for democracy:

> *The marketplace of ideas will often fail to produce the truth. ... some kind of chilling effect on false statements of fact is important – not only to protect people against negligence, cruelty and unjustified damage to their reputations – but also to ensure the proper functioning of democracy itself*[3]

The principle of a right to be forgotten enjoys support from a majority of EU governments and – quite probably – of EU citizens. This support comes from the gradual realisation that the internet sweeps up and distributes information which crosses a barrier between the private and personal. As Matthias Moulin of the French data protection authority explained:

> People have been waiting for such a right. The internet has been a real revelation for access to information. It is immediate, worldwide, accessible. The professional and non-professional are all mixed up. It sweeps up too much, giving opportunities for new kinds of bad behaviour. We need a quality of balance between the good and bad. The law was not adapted and had to rebalance.[4]

The right to be forgotten tries to convert the twentieth-century doctrine of data protection to new circumstances, unforeseen when data protection first took shape. When the current EU directive on data came into force in 1998, fewer than 10 per cent of the Union's citizens were connected to the internet. The collision between old rules and new purposes lies at the root of many of the problems with the right to be forgotten. The European Court judgment which gave the idea such a boost was a groundbreaking one for the information age. Whether it can or will set a lasting precedent is another question.

Discovering search

Humans now store, search, and retrieve information which is held both online and offline: we all have hybrid sources of information, freely mixing online and offline. The store of online information may be vast, but it still rests on, and is built above, knowledge accumulated and recorded in the pre-digital age. We can only reach it by links. 'The hyperlink is one of the primary vehicles of the Internet's unprecedented ability to connect people with ideas and information.'[5] But our curiosity about how those connections are made is only beginning to catch up with our prolific use of links. As Julia Powles, an academic lawyer, puts it:

> We have come to rely, comprehensively and largely unwittingly, on privately-owned, culturally biased, black box services in navigating the digital ecosystem and discovering and reconstructing information. We have outsourced the raw material, design and execution of multi-layered search strategies, in return for easy, efficient interfaces and mysterious algorithms.[6]

Internet companies driven by software engineers have been first and foremost explorers of what is possible and what will work; they have worked empirically and by improvisation. Companies such as Google which have grown to become large and powerful are sometimes seen through a false perspective which assumes that their expansion was planned and executed to follow a strategy formed from the start.

That assumption cannot survive reading any account, written from the outside or inside, of the early years of a corporation like Google. The founders and their early colleagues were making things up as they went along. They had big, long-range aims but did not debate every angle and possible consequence. Innovators rarely do. Google staff may have been told not to do 'evil', but that mission is abstract; information technology is detailed, specific, and, like anything else, has unintended and unforeseen consequences.

Pioneer Silicon Valley companies tended to launch a product first and then subsequently to debate and to discover what people thought. As a critic once said of Facebook, the company is better at asking forgiveness than at asking permission. Google's founders and engineers were genuinely startled to find that failing to allow early users of Gmail a 'delete' button enraged many of those people. The company backed off and allowed deletion. Google landed itself in a long lawsuit when it announced its plan to digitise the world's published books with barely any prior consultation with book publishers.

Much of the profitability of companies like Google is derived from combining agile, fast algorithms with what amount to huge do-it-yourself market surveys. The result is to make meaning out of heterogeneous fragments. The market research is supplied by users themselves uploading pictures and words, as for example on Facebook, or entering search queries, as on Google, Yahoo, or Bing. Facebook learns about the lives and preferences of its users by analysing the content they themselves supply. The aggregated data produce group or individual advertising targets. Google does not make money from search queries. Income arrives from advertisers who can target Google users with data derived from billions of searches. And not just advertisers: credit and insurance companies, to name only two data-hungry industries, have an almost limitless appetite for information on any detail of a person's life which equips them to make a subtler or more authoritative judgement about someone's risk for credit or insurance. 'All data is credit data,' says Douglas Merrill, a former chief information officer at Google who wants to reform the assessment of credit risk for the information-rich age.[7]

'Machine learning', a branch of artificial intelligence, deploys algorithms which are programmed to seek out, without further human intervention, ways to improve the data analysis, to gather further data, and to improve on the improvements. Google currently processes, worldwide, 40,000 searches per second, over 3.5 billion a day and 1.2 trillion in a year. The company had been in existence for more than a decade before it admitted that it had stored a record of every search ever requested. The internet scholar Lawrence Lessig defined Google's core business like this:

> They have produced this amazing machine for building data, and that data has its own 'network effect' – the more people who use it, the more data generated, the more advertisers flock to it. Everything sits on top of that layer, starting with search. Every time you search, you give Google some value because you pick a certain result. Every time you pick a result, Google learns something from that.[8]

Google therefore has a strong economic interest in the fullest and most up-to-date results data possible and a corresponding stake in resisting limits on search.

Data protection

The idea of 'data protection' came into existence to extend and update the older and elusive idea of privacy to deal with twentieth-century fears and technology. The single most famous argument for privacy law ever written was in part provoked by the arrival of cheap cameras on the mass market in America. 'Instantaneous photographs and newspaper enterprise have invaded the sacred precincts of private and domestic life,' wrote the American lawyers Samuel Warren and Louis Brandeis in 1890, 'and numerous mechanical devices threaten to make good the prediction that "what is whispered in the closet shall be proclaimed from the house-tops."' The cameras they had in mind were 'snap' cameras invented by the Eastman Kodak company which made photography no longer something which required large and expensive equipment. They defined privacy as the 'right to be let alone' and a 'general right to the immunity of the person, the right to one's personality'. Those latter phrases were, in fact, more in tune with ideas held in parts of Europe than in the US. To this day, while American law contains several measures protecting personal information and there is a privacy tort, there is no general law of privacy.

Britain did not pass such a privacy law until 1998[9] but most other European states had done so earlier. Privacy was a flexible and broad catchall term long before frictionless and intimate digital publishing began to change practices and attitudes. Privacy was often defined in terms of space: the right to keep one's home from being inspected or snooped on or the control of filing cabinets containing sensitive details. But is the test of whether something is private a right to be left alone, to be able to limit access to oneself, to keep certain things secret (even when in the hands of others), to have control over one's image, reputation, or dignity (in the public domain) or the protection of intimacy? The development of 'data protection' separate from the defence of privacy in Europe was in part an attempt to escape the complexities of overlapping but different philosophies of privacy.

Ideas and intuitions about privacy have many overlapping layers; there is no settled definition.[10] In Europe in the middle of the twentieth century, the most widespread privacy worries were about the power of the state to misuse information on individuals. Towards the end of the century, those anxieties were joined by fears of powerful mass media in private hands and the invasive risks of digital communication.

Those fears focused on the intimidating power of digital memory, which could be powerful enough to constitute a 'chilling effect' of its own. 'Everything you've ever posted online could come back to haunt you someday,' one far-sighted prophet wrote in 1998.[11] The free flow of information might have benefits but could itself become a constraint in twenty-first-century conditions, this argument ran. Blog posts or fragments of video could attract huge audiences within minutes or hours. Cybercrowds might be appreciative or neutral but, cut off from face-to-face contact, the ability to verify, and knowledge of context, they could become mobs determined to shame an individual.

Dimensions of privacy

Not only are ideas about privacy enormously varied between different national cultures, but laws and social conventions about privacy are dynamic. Beliefs about what is private shift over time. In Western societies, for example, the limits of privacy around sex have moved towards greater openness. Technology can move the frontier between what can be kept private and what can't; users of new services and social networks can choose to surrender privacy in exchange for benefits. The snap camera which worried Warren and Brandeis offered the same combination of threat and promise as smartphone cameras and Instagram do today. Few technology company CEOs are as blunt as Scott McNealy of Sun Microsystems who said in 1999: 'You have zero privacy anyway. Get over it.'[12]

From the 1970s, the long-standing debate over privacy among lawyers and scholars acquired a new concern. Ideas about data protection focused not on the gathering of information or its distribution, but on the processing. Was personal information being used for purposes other than those for which it had been collected in the first place? Computers increased that risk.

In Europe in the 1970s and 1980s, judges and policymakers were unsure about whether data protection was a kind of privacy or a separate right. Ideas about how far the protection of privacy should extend anyway varied from society to society. In continental legal traditions, privacy was expanded by the 'right of personality'. A French court in 1970 laid down that a new privacy provision in the civil code covered 'the right to one's name, one's image, one's intimacy, one's honour and reputation, one's own biography and the right to have one's past transgressions forgotten'.[13]

The European Court of Human Rights tended to see data protection as a new dimension of privacy. Elsewhere and gradually, data protection came to be seen as a separate set of ideas, if not a right. An important decision by the German Constitutional Court in 1983 stressed 'informational autonomy' or 'informational self-determination'. The Council of Europe first passed a resolution on the right to be protected from unauthorised processing of personal data in 1981. This idea extended well beyond the idea of privacy as the insulation of the personal or intimate: professional, published, and commercial data might be covered.

Data protection is little understood partly because, while the law's theoretical powers are sweeping, they have been little-used until recently. The law was drawn with wide scope by EU lawmakers in the 1990s attempting, with limited success, to create a template which would cover many varieties of anxiety about personal information.

Europe's memories

The largest of those fears is the use of data by totalitarian governments. Nazi Germany was nothing if not systematic and thorough in its information control, not only of Germans but also of conquered populations. In the 1930s, the Dutch government had compiled an unprecedentedly full registry of facts about its own citizens. Driven by the need to plan public welfare schemes which were then becoming increasingly popular, the Dutch government listed everyone by name, date of birth, address, and religion. Few, if any, other European states held complete information of this sort as accurate or as up to date. For the German occupation forces, identifying and finding Jews and gypsies was made easy. Seventy per cent of the Dutch Jews died, most in concentration camps, compared to 25 per cent in France and 40 per cent in Belgium.

For East Germans, the even more thorough Stasi replaced the Nazi state. Central and Eastern Europe along with Russia suffered the same under Stalin and his successors. The reunification of Germany from 1989 and the revelations of the depth, breadth, and scale of secret knowledge held by the state in the East only served to consolidate suspicion of unsupervised data collection and use. In Central Africa, every citizen of Rwanda had been required, under laws framed by the Belgian colonial rulers of the country, to carry an identity card which listed their ethnic origin. When inter-ethnic tensions turned murderous in 1994, that information contributed to the deaths of tens of thousands of Tutsis, easily identified by the Hutu militias which manned roadblocks at which the passes would be inspected.

These fears underlie much of the drive after World War II in Europe to give individuals ownership or control of personal information. The worries were largely focused on the powers of the state and what could be done with information held in filing cabinets. American ideas about privacy were largely either about sector-specific problems such as privacy of medical records or creditworthiness data and about keeping the government out of your home. In Europe, there had been a few attempts to establish codes for the fair use and protection of personal information in the 1970s (in Sweden and the German state of Hesse). The German Constitutional Court in 1983 laid down a new doctrine which fused two ideas: that privacy is essential to the exercise of autonomy and free will and that to feel fully autonomous an individual is entitled to know what information is held about him or her.

The court said:

> *The freedom of the individual to decide on himself is at stake when the individual is uncertain about what is known about him, particularly*

> where what society might view as deviant behaviour is at stake (the chilling effect). The individual therefore has a right to know and to decide on information being processed about him.[14]

German data protection law was strengthened as a result. By the 1990s, the German government among others was keen to see data protection law at pan-European level. Among other reasons, businesses were keen to make data flows across borders easier in parallel to the liberalisation of telecommunications. But the heart of the matter was competing claims about what best protects an individual's autonomy. In the more recent words of Paul Nemitz, the European Commission official in overall charge of data protection, the internet's bright moving spotlight of attention is a 'chilling effect' in its own right which qualifies claims for freedoms of expression or knowledge: 'What chilling effect is bigger? If we are able to know everything about you? ... Or whether we allow individuals to have control over their data?'[15]

Elsewhere on the continent more stress was laid on the defence of personal identity and reputation rather than on autonomy. In 1985 the Italian supreme court first affirmed a *diritto all'oblio* (right to be forgotten) in a judgment which said that someone as an 'essential part of his personality, has the right not to have his intellectual, political, social, religious and professional heritage misrepresented'. This was linked to each person's right to be unique and to defend the combination of unique characteristics and attributes they wish to project to other people and in the media.[16] This right overlaps with defamation, but is not the same thing. The French version of the right to be forgotten (*droit à l'oubli*) appeared in 1966, in a commentary on a decision by a Paris court of the previous year.

In 1978 France had passed a law on computing and data storage which did not mention the right to be forgotten in so many words but which laid down a right to rectify or erase personal information which was 'inaccurate, incomplete, ambiguous, out of date', or which could not legally be gathered or retained. That language is similar to wording which began to appear in data protection laws in Europe, eventually in the EU directive and elsewhere in the world.

These very broad definitions of enforceable rights to inspect, correct, or erase information held or published about a person had origins in the defence of reputation, a cause which resonates particularly strongly in France, Spain, and Italy. What is sometimes described in Germany as the right to 'informational self-determination' is more often described to the south as the right to one's image, honour, dignity, name, or reputation. It is a right to retain the respect of others by controlling what people can say about you. Legal rights of privacy and data protection are seen as rules for civilised behaviour. Some elements of this are derived from 'rights' once only enjoyed by aristocrats and princes, now extended to all citizens. Both the Polish and Russian constitutions protect not only the right to defend one's reputation but also 'honour'.

This is a paradox: a right to privacy is seen as a right to a public face. When French press law began to be liberalised in the 1820s, the defenders of that change insisted that press freedom was only for the public sphere. Private life was 'walled off' and facts about private life, true or not, could not legally be printed. One historian of this trend wrote that 'the importance of the protection of "honourable" privacy was something close to orthodoxy in France by the 1890s'.[17]

In France and elsewhere, the idea of controlling one's image also included the law's help in restarting with a clean slate. Continental jurisdictions vary greatly in the way this operates, but most grant some accused and some convicted anonymity or the opportunity to have reporting of convictions later erased. In 2013, a French court ordered the withdrawal of a book and fined a publisher and photographer, Yan Morvan, for breaching a person's right to control an image. The book, about gangs, reproduced a picture of a far-right activist given the name 'Petit Mathieu' taken more than 20 years before and not identified in the text. Petit Mathieu, by then a man in his forties, sued and won. Britain, on a much more limited front, has allowed the expunging of spent convictions for certain, less serious offences for more than 40 years and provides anonymity under certain conditions for those accused of rape.

Different philosophies

Reflecting both uncertainty and gulfs between cultures, judgments about the control of reputation and image showed inconsistent patterns between states and sometimes between courts in the same state. The data protection head for Hamburg remarked at a Cambridge conference in 2015 that the philosophy behind data protection remained an 'alien concept' in parts of the EU.[18] In 2006 the Frankfurt high court acknowledged a general right to be forgotten but refused a request from a prisoner to edit a newspaper archive on account of his lengthy years in prison and lack of interest in rehabilitation. A year later the Hamburg high court allowed a request from a prisoner, finding that

> the interest in rehabilitation did outweigh the interest of the archive in being complete. It therefore had to delete the plaintiff's name from its publications. Furthermore, concerning the potential harm articles on convicted persons can have on their rehabilitation, the court found that monitoring its archives in order to prevent infringements of the right of oblivion seems to be a reasonable obligation for an online archive.[19]

Meanwhile American law developed in another direction. The power of the First Amendment to the constitution (forbidding restraints on free speech and the press) and the lack of any explicit privacy right in the constitution made privacy harder to enforce. What leverage the law did provide was gradually reduced by an exemption for 'newsworthiness' which grew stronger in the twentieth century. Beyond limited instances such as medical confidentiality, courts were reluctant to extend privacy protection to information which had been published and which was true. When Sara Jane Moore tried to assassinate US President Gerald Ford in 1975, she was tackled by an ex-Marine called Oliver Sipple. Sipple pleaded, unsuccessfully, with reporters and politicians who were congratulating him not to reveal that he was gay; his family did not know. He sued a San Francisco paper for invasion of privacy but lost. The court held that there was a legitimate news interest in his private life and that he had not made it secret. Many years later, Sipple committed suicide.

Continental European cultural traditions are imprinted on the laws and attitudes of today – but in a patchwork miscellany which reflects national experience and legal evolution. French and Italian courts were sympathetic to the idea of a person being able make a claim to erase information causing damage or distress before data protection laws (which allowed the same thing) arrived. Swedish law permits the existence of an open database which carries comprehensive listing of criminal convictions. Two different ideas lie behind these variations. Most European jurisdictions allow some form of 'clean slate' fresh start for people convicted, at least of minor offences. But obscuring criminal convictions is extended in some legal philosophies to be part of redemption or forgiveness.

Two years before the Google Spain judgment, an Italian case saw the tradition of image protection law applied in the digital age. News publications carry news which changes but also hold easily retrievable archives. Does the ease of retrieving old news impose a new duty on news publishers to keep old information updated? If the law sees the presentation of personality as important, it can do. But it will depend on which court in Europe is deciding the case.

A local politician in Italy arrested for corruption in 1993 sued a major newspaper some years later for keeping available a record of the arrest without ever reporting that he had not been convicted. The politician lost the case before both the Italian data protection authority and a court in Milan. But he won in the supreme court, which declared that the right to be forgotten encompassed a right to require a newspaper report shown to be incomplete or outdated to be updated. The Italian supreme court has made two judgments of this kind and they have been criticised for imposing a heavy burden on news organisations. So far the burden appears to be theoretical; there has been no sign of Italian online news archives being searched to discover if they are sufficiently up to date. In 2009, the German Constitutional Court was asked a similar question and clarified that websites are not obliged to permanently check their archives for compliance with anonymity rights of people convicted of crimes.[20]

The European Court of Human Rights has also tended to take a cautious line on balancing the public's right of access to information and the protection of reputation. In a Polish case, the judges came down against altering information in the public domain, stressing that

> *It is not the role of judicial authorities to engage in rewriting history by ordering the removal from the public domain of all traces of publications which have in the past been found, by final judicial decisions, to amount to unjustified attacks on individual reputations.*
>
> *… it is relevant for the assessment of the case that the legitimate interest of the public in access to the public Internet archives of the press is protected under Article 10 of the Convention.*[21]

More than a hundred countries have passed some version of data protection laws.[22] The laws aim to provide a framework of duties for any organisation's handling of personal or sensitive data. They allow a citizen to inspect his or her data and apply to fix an error. In the early years of the new millennium, when the first rush of enthusiasm for internet technology had begun to wear off, the pressure to be able to fix problems was rising. The claim by high-tech giants like Google that they were merely operating automatic processing operations which involved no discretion, intervention, or judgement of any human kind was also looking increasingly implausible. The corollary of their claim only to be the stewards of algorithms – the implication that they bore no responsibility for the outcomes of the information processing they performed – has gradually become untenable.

Until 2014 some search engines hoped and thought that they were protected by the EU 'e-commerce directive',[23] which limits liability for internet platforms such as internet service providers which are technical carriers with no knowledge of the content they host. Regulators and policymakers were unsure about how to classify businesses like Google and Facebook. Are they utilities, under private ownership but supplying such basic needs on such a scale that they require regulation as gas, electric, or telephone companies once were? Are they equivalent – because of their importance to all forms of democratic, social, and commercial communication – to a public service broadcaster? Or are they simply the innovative leaders of a modern phenomenon, 'information capitalism'?[24]

Google is very much more than a search engine. Revelations about the links between Google's search and advertising business undermined the claim that Google is the modern equivalent of the Dewey Decimal book indexing system, postmodern hip librarians doing no more than organising the world's information. Google's information-indexing, however widely used and useful, is a database run by a for-profit company. The scale and success of Google and Facebook in particular ensured a much deeper scrutiny, wider debate, scepticism, and, among some European political classes, outright hostility. Google, seen largely in its early years as benevolent and inventive, began to feature in dystopian fiction. Dave Eggers's 2010 novel *The Circle* is set in a lightly disguised Google, a corporation run by people in energetic denial about the extent of the company's information-shaping power and its capacity to do wrong despite good intentions.

A search engine's 'autocomplete' function is an example of the mismatch of intentions and outcomes in law. Words and phrases pop up automatically, but they suggest an editorial hand at work. In countries with laws protecting 'personality rights', these can almost cause more trouble than the archived information itself. In 2010, the regional court of Paris decided in favour of a plaintiff who wanted to stop Google spelling out 'rapist', 'sentenced', and 'satanist' when his name was in the search box, although these terms were accurate references to reporting of his past. The court argued that algorithms were based on human thought and that to have a defence Google would have to prove that autocomplete statements were not made by the company. In 2011, the Hamburg high court, faced with a libel case brought by an estate agency whose name brought up 'fraud', found that the algorithm was not Google's opinion and that it did not have the duty to filter each autocomplete wording.

The officials at CNIL, France's data protection authority, noticed that complaints asking for information either to be taken down or obscured began to rise between 2010 and 2012. 'There was pent-up demand,' said Matthias Moulin, CNIL's deputy director, 'and the right to be forgotten judgment answered a real concern, particularly about correcting social networks and blogs. Before the Google Spain decision, ordinary people with no public position could ask for something to be taken down or delisted and they knew they wouldn't succeed.'[25]

CNIL had tried, in alliance with the relevant government minister, to broker a self-regulation system for internet companies, but it was voluntary and did not capture some of the largest. In 2007, the Spanish AEPD had issued a policy paper on search engines and privacy law which argued that the search companies were significant processors of data and arguing for international standards of privacy protection to apply to them.[26] Appearing before a committee of legislators, the AEPD director made a significant distinction. Personal information harvested by search engines, he said, 'may be legitimate at source, [but] its universal and secular conservation on the internet may be disproportionate'.[27] Spanish law was toughened to encourage people to ask for links to be removed or information erased. By the following year, the AEPD had more than a hundred dissatisfied complainants whose claims had been refused. One was Sr Costeja of Barcelona.

European policymakers want the EU to been seen as a global influence on privacy and data protection and stress the differences between the EU and the world's outlier in data protection, the US. Europe, this narrative says, has made smooth and steady progress towards better protecting its citizens by gradually strengthening an individual's control of their personal information. A middle ground is being carved out between 'information anarchy and censorship'.[28] The EU has the best of these laws in the world, the Commissioner in charge said in 2010.[29] Progress, albeit slow, is being made updating data protection for the twenty-first century.

This is better than America, where government policy is over-influenced by the high-tech giants of Silicon Valley and where privacy laws are scattered and incoherent. What better evidence could there be of Europe's agenda-setting power than the spread of data protection laws across the globe?

This is a reassuring story, but self-deceiving. Underlying the apparently well-ordered field of data protection is an ill-matched collection of ideas which have not been welded into a clear set of specific remedies for identifiable harms, a weak commitment to respect the right to freedom of expression, and risks that a ratchet effect will expand opportunities to delete or amend the public record. There is no question that cheap processors, sensors, and servers have produced a volume of accumulated, preserved information from which inaccurate, distressing, or damaging information can be instantly retrieved. How best to deal with that new dilemma has not yet been properly addressed anywhere. The failure to address the heart of the issue is, at least in part, because European data protection law is not fit for twenty-first-century purposes.

3

Striking the Balance

Digital and internet communications have refashioned the routes along which information travels, the conditions under which it is stored, and helped to create new entities which control its distribution. All societies face the task of adapting conventions, norms, and laws to apply timeless values and principles to new conditions. How well adapted are the ideas and law of data protection in general and the right to be forgotten in particular to this new context?

Balance of rights

Human rights codes do not usually rank basic rights by priority. Fundamental rights are supposed to have equal force and where they are found in conflict, they are weighed according to the facts of a case. From the outset, European data protection assumed a superior right to amend, delete, or obscure information and specifies conditions under which this will apply. The right to information, free speech, or free expression entered the original laws as exemptions, if at all, not as rights which are to be balanced. In some states, these rights have been robustly defended by courts and by data protection authorities. Freedom of speech and expression is supposed to be safeguarded by national courts which have discretion to define the precise scope of this exception to the more powerful rights of the 'data subject'. But national courts are faced with the difficulty of interpreting a basic design of the law which treats rights asymmetrically in the first place.

Current EU law on data makes an exception for what is phrased as 'journalistic purposes or for artistic or literary expression'. Sweden, Finland, and Denmark give a wide interpretation to freedom of speech defences. Swedish data protection law simply, and without qualification, says that the country's two laws guaranteeing freedom of expression outrank the data protection statute. The Swedish high court rejected on appeal a complaint about a blogger who had been alleging banking malpractice, confirming that the journalism exemption (in data protection law) covered all forms of comment on matters of public importance.[1]

The formula of giving protection to 'journalistic' publishing is itself a problem in the digital age. Journalism was once easy to recognise and identify. In the era of printed newspapers and terrestrial television, news media employing journalists were quasi-industrial enterprises. Digital technology has spread the ability to publish to anyone with a smartphone. Narrow definitions of 'journalism' tend to restrict what can be protected: the law should rather protect disclosure in the public interest and not hinge on the professional identification of the person making the disclosure. Revelations do not always depend solely on people who would identify themselves, or be identified as, journalists. Important roles can be played by whistleblowers, witnesses, activists, bloggers, or go-betweens. The boundaries around journalism may always have been porous, but there are no professional boundaries now. Is a site which rates local authorities or councillors 'journalistic'? Or a site which maps crimes? Is Facebook, which provides platforms specifically for news publishing? In the latter case, Facebook is quite clearly involved in an editorial process which selects news to present, albeit one which combines human judgement and algorithmic automation.[2] All these sites process data and all generate knowledge which can claim to be in the public interest. Interpreting current EU law, the European Court has varied its interpretation of the journalistic exemption, tending over time to narrow its use. There has been very little definition of what 'literary or artistic purposes' might cover in practice.

The data protection scholar David Erdos has analysed the freedom of speech protections in data protection laws across the EU since the first directive came into force in 1998. When the exemptions for journalism, literary, and artistic activities first came to be tested by the EU court in 2008, the court underlined the rights liable to be in conflict and stressed the 'importance of the right to freedom of expression', adding that it would interpret terms such as journalism 'broadly'. But doubt remained. Erdos quotes a senior official at the UK Information Commissioner's office as saying that the exemptions did not apply 'in general for freedom of expression', but were only for 'what you might broadly call the media'.[3] That leaves many communications which might have public value outside a definition of journalism, literature, or art.

Rating websites might be one example. Some are malicious and some produce information which many people find useful. They are all 'processing' data. The French data protection authority CNIL received

160 complaints about a teacher rating website called Note2be.com and investigated. They found that the site was committing several legal breaches at once. It could easily be confused with an official site when in fact it was a private sector business. Under data protection law, the teachers were entitled to be asked to give their consent to be rated and had not. The site had no 'legitimate interest' which would allow it to evade that requirement. There was no way a user of the site could 'verify' the quality of the judgements. The case went to court and appeal judges, ordering the site closed, added that the site's operators had failed to ensure the 'adequacy' and 'relevance' of their information.

That ruling is worth spelling out because it illustrates very clearly how a law dealing with how data may or may not be processed comes to be used to control information and content in the public sphere. A law originally designed to regulate the bilateral relationship between a (probably more powerful) company or state and the person about whom it held information has gradually become a means of determining what information circulates in a democracy. Not very long after the French cases above, the German courts were asked to rule on a German teacher-rating site, spickmich.de. A number of complaints had been brought under both privacy and data protection law. The Federal Court eventually found the site to be legal, not only stressing the importance of taking freedom of expression into account, but also noting that the site was subscriber-only. This did not leave the law clear.

Information publishing or disclosing deserves a full free expression defence in new data protection law. If that is considered too broad and liable to abuse, the defence can be qualified by protecting the publishing or disclosure of information of public value or in the public interest. Both an exemption for 'exercising the right of freedom of expression and information' and for data processing 'carried out in the public interest' are included in the new EU data protection law. That language is welcome and stronger than the current version, but its exact interpretation by courts is yet to be seen.[4]

Scope and language

The committee of EU data protection authorities, when considering the application of law to social networking sites, came to the conclusion that if people wish to upload pictures 'or information about other individuals' this should be done with the consent of the individual concerned.[5] EU law provides a 'household exemption' for everyday personal activity, but different courts have set the boundaries for this in different places. One court found that posting a tagged old school photograph without consent on a Polish social network was illegal processing of personal data.[6] Data law classifies information about 'racial or ethnic origin' as especially sensitive and subject to special restrictions. Court judgments have held that colour photographs fall inside this definition because they can reveal race or ethnicity.[7]

The incoming EU law[8] includes guidance which defines 'personal and household activities' as those which are not professional or commercial (and thus exempt) while putting 'controllers and processors which provide the means for processing personal data' under the law.[9] Again, it remains to be seen whether courts can reconcile this distinction with everyday activity online.

The scope of data protection law will remain wide. It was not until the Google Spain case in 2014, examined in detail in the next chapter, that it became clear how EU law applied to search engines and a right to be forgotten. In the years since the EU's directive was passed in 1995, search engines had become the principal tool for using the internet. Search engines like Google, Yahoo, Bing, Dogpile, and DuckDuckGo were certainly processing data; most were storing it.

The tension between slowly evolving and clarifying law and rapidly innovating technology means that the right to be forgotten covers several quite distinct meanings and purposes. As a result, original purposes are distorted or expanded. When the right to be forgotten was first picked up and mentioned by an EU Commissioner, there was a hint that it was confined to social media posts made, and later regretted, by individuals. Announcing that the right would make an appearance in a revised data protection law, Viviane Reding said:

> Social network sites are a great way to stay in touch with friends and share information. But if people no longer want to use a service, they should have no problem wiping out their profiles. The right to be forgotten is particularly relevant to personal data that is no longer needed for the purposes for which it was collected.[10]

That could be described as the easiest version of a right to be forgotten. It would also be a practical way of rewriting the rights of access and correction already in data protection law for the Facebook age. Someone who has posted information of their own about themselves on a network wants to delete it. Not all social networks grant this immediately and there may be arguments about the lingering retention of data, but most major social networks now allow people to do this. Google offers users the ability to inspect and delete their search history while warning that the company may 'store activity separately to prevent spam and abuse and to improve our services'. A law to enforce a person's right to remove information about themselves from public view on a site on which they had posted it in the first place is not likely to be controversial. (A law to force networks to delete it completely would be controversial and contested.)

But the right to be forgotten stretches much further. The blending of privacy (in the wide continental sense of reputation control) and data protection rights has taken the right to the point where it is interpreted as a right to delete information about oneself, published by someone else and which may have been legitimately published and (or) true – and without any requirement to show harm or distress. By the time the mission creep has gone that far, freedom of expression is at some risk.

This would be enough of a problem if the criteria for erasing or obscuring information were clear. They are not. Again, these are sweeping theoretical powers where more discriminate and specific ones would make the balancing of competing rights easier to accomplish. Article 6 of the first, current EU directive (on which national laws are based) is titled 'Principles relating to data quality'. The key clauses say that personal data must be:

> (a) *adequate, relevant and not excessive in relation to the purposes for which they are collected and/or further processed;*
> (b) *accurate and, where necessary, kept up to date; every reasonable step must be taken to ensure that data which are inaccurate or incomplete, having regard to the purposes for which they were collected or for which they are further processed, are erased or rectified.*

Law is often worded broadly and flexibly to allow for detailed interpretation by courts or to allow for possible changes in circumstance. But the attempt to provide a template covering the countries of the EU (15 in 1995, now 28) has used terms so flexible that subsequent interpretation has not made matters clearer. The text above was reproduced, more or less, in 28 national data protection laws. Disputes in an individual country are settled by either the data protection authority or a court. In the case of Sr Costeja, the opinion of the European Court was asked. The court said, for example, that information should not be de-indexed by a search engine if it concerned a 'public figure'. That new nuance of interpretation was picked up by the EU data protection authorities who looked at the operation of the request handling in the year after Google Spain and found that most refusals 'directly related to the professional activity of the individual'.[11] That was a slightly different criterion again. Investigative journalists would often argue that information which they gather may be classified as either professional or private, but either can have a claim to be disclosed in the public interest.[12]

In a world of public and government authorities which stored your details in filing cabinets and where memories of totalitarian governments were fresh, broad phrasing made sense. The amount of information likely to trouble the definitions was small. In an information-rich world with instant, frictionless retrieval and potentially indefinite preservation of data, subjective and nebulous words like 'adequate' or 'relevant' (to what or to whom?) are merely the start of long arguments. Even 'accurate' and 'up to date' are not easily agreed. As we will see in the next chapter, the language of the EU Court in the Google Spain case was no more precise.

The 'ratchet effect'

The importance of free speech and the right to know are deeply embedded in European culture. European law has not developed as American law has done under the strong influence of the First Amendment. But free expression appears in legal codes and constitutions and is the subject of ceaseless debate. Against that background, it remains mysterious that European law has developed in data protection a doctrine which treats freedom of speech so superficially. The risk is not as alarming or immediate as some critics of the right to be forgotten have claimed. But the cumulative development of data protection, the Google Spain judgment and its implementation, and the upcoming rewrite of EU law[13] (incorporating a right to be forgotten) have created a momentum towards de-indexing and deletion which is a danger. It has created expectations beyond those which data law should be able to achieve. The danger is not of a censorship regime or of 'deleting history' on any scale, but of ratchet moves which gradually extend the law's grasp.

This is not a popular argument. The risks of small ratchet moves are seen by advocates of stronger data protection as insignificant in the context of the huge high-tech forces driving towards greater transparency. The high-tech giants are suspected of wielding too much power over people and even over governments. They are suspected of being too helpful to governments, and particularly to Washington, in allowing covert agencies to spy on communications. They have been careless with the unintended consequences of data processing for too long. The moral force behind legal restraint on data processing is understandable.

But when data processing law collides with the newest technology, perverse and inconsistent results occur. Digital communications are an engine of opportunity: they have and will enable people to invent new ways of communicating, processing data, and using them for myriad purposes. The internet is not a democratic institution; it is a neutral network which can be used for bad just as for good. Yet it is now also the most important element of the infrastructure of free expression.

The argument for free expression is not a coded appeal for the news media alone, although journalists have felt the effect of the right to be forgotten.[14] Public debate, the quality of public reason, education, the historical record, innovation, invention, civic life, and the maximisation of the potential of each person all depend on the most open communication which we can manage and is compatible with avoiding harm. The defence of free speech on the internet must prevent the erosion of communications freedom by insisting on specific and proportionate remedies for identifiable wrongs. Data protection, rebranded as the right to be forgotten and however well-intentioned and sincere, carries the risk of shrinking and chilling free expression.

4

Google Spain

Mario Costeja Gonzalez did not like googling himself. He disliked anybody doing it. A search on his name told anyone who looked that, in 1998, some of his property had been compulsorily sold to pay social security debts. So irritated was he by this that he changed a single letter in the spelling of his name on his business card to frustrate anyone searching for him on the web. In 2009 he sent complaints to *La Vanguardia*, the Barcelona newspaper which had published the auction announcements, and to Google the following year. Getting no satisfaction, he contacted the AEPD, Spain's data protection authority.

Europe's data protection commissioners were already taking an interest in search engines. Their spring conference in 2007 heard from an Italian data commissioner that the internet was 'doing away with space and time limits in the dissemination of information' and that this was a 'violation' of the 'right to oblivion', a right achieved in earlier practice not by deletion but by the difficulties of finding anything in a dusty newspaper archive. The Italian data protection authority, the Garante, was negotiating with Google to sort out the problem.[1]

At the end of that year, the AEPD issued a paper on search engines which argued that search engines should be held liable for their data processing of information about individuals. Publishers of original material might be able to claim freedom of information rights, but search engines could not. A few months later, the EU data protection authorities published their opinion that, while privacy and the protection of personal data had to be balanced against the free flow of information, that balance applied only to 'the media', implying that search engines did not belong in that protected category.

The AEPD's director, Artemi Rallo Lombarte, clarified that while publishers might be able to refuse erasure requests, search engines could not object to the less severe sanction of de-indexing. The AEPD increased its adjudications against Google, requiring removal of links to around a hundred newspaper articles and also announcements in the Official Gazette. Google refused, citing along other arguments the 'profound chilling effect' which delisting would have on free speech. In January 2011 Google appealed five test cases to the high court in Madrid. Sr Costeja's case was then referred by the Spanish judges to the EU judges for a precedent-setting decision.

The EU court in Luxembourg was asked to answer three questions:

1. Was a search engine such as Google, headquartered outside the EU but with subsidiaries operating inside, within the scope of the data protection directive?
2. Does Google 'process' information and is it a 'data controller'?
3. Does the *derecho al olvido* (right to be forgotten) extend as far as allowing someone to apply to a search engine to have information 'consigned to oblivion', even though the information in question has been lawfully published by third parties?

The case was heard in 2013. Having read the most closely comparable cases which had gone to the court since the directive had been passed, most participants believed that the central issue was the balance of competing rights. The Austrian government argued to the court that the right to erase a reference to a person or a link to it depended on whether the information had already been found wrong or unlawful. The European Commission, then wrestling with the revision of the directive that was being interpreted by the court, and supported by Poland, argued that the claim for delisting was weak. To argue that a link was merely 'prejudicial' was not enough.

Google lawyers and advisers believed that the facts of the Costeja case helped: the original publication was uncontroversial and the facts supplied by a government body. There was no question of libel. They did not intend to argue that they were a media organisation, because a search engine does not create editorial content, and they did not think that they needed to claim a 'journalistic' purpose exemption. But they did tell the court that to impose 'data controller' obligations on a search engine would chill free expression.

EU court judgments are preceded by a preliminary opinion from an Advocate-General. The Google team felt even better when the court's Advocate-General issued his written finding. Those views are not binding on the court, but they are often followed, wholly or in part. Niilo Jääskinen, the Finnish Advocate-General, began by noting that the directive which the court was being asked to clarify was now operating in a world quite different from the one which existed when it was written. 'Nowadays,' he wrote, 'almost anyone with a smartphone or computer could be considered to be engaged in activities on the internet to which the Directive could potentially apply'.[2]

The development of the internet into a 'comprehensive global stock of information' had not been foreseen by the EU's lawmakers. The broad definitions of data and processing in the directive were likely to apply to an 'unprecedentedly' wide range of new situations. The court therefore should use 'proportionality' as a guide to avoid 'unreasonable and excessive legal consequences'. A proportionate balance, Jääskinen continued, needed to be struck between four things: the protection of personal data, the objectives of the information society, the interests of economic operators, and, last but not least, internet users.

Google's operations did fall, he found, under EU law but he did not think that it qualified as what the directive terms a 'data controller'. The third question on a possible 'right to be forgotten' raised questions of competing fundamental rights. The directive did not give a general or absolute right to be forgotten. The proposed revision of EU data protection law, he noted in a loaded paragraph, did include the right but as a 'legal innovation' and it had 'met with considerable opposition'.

Jääskinen quoted from the judgments of the European Court of Human Rights[3] on the right to seek information and free access to it. A search engine exercised a lawful right to conduct business and to freedom of expression. 'Imbuing' the directive with a right to be forgotten 'would entail sacrificing pivotal rights such as freedom of expression and information'. He also warned the court against saddling the search engines with the obligation to sit in judgment on delisting requests. They would be particularly hard to judge because, if a right to be forgotten were to be allowed, the companies would have to evaluate requests for 'suppressing legitimate and legal information that has entered the public sphere'.

A month after the Advocate-General's opinion appeared, the Snowden revelations of industrial-scale electronic surveillance began, implicating not only the US and UK governments in covert eavesdropping but embroiling American high-tech companies, including Google, in claims that they had cooperated in secret.

In their reply to the Advocate-General's arguments, the judges in their final decision did not merely disagree. They rejected his whole approach. Having determined that Google fell within EU law and counted as a data controller, they focused strictly on the wording of the data protection directive. The radically increased quantity of information and access to it presents individuals with new threats because of the ease of processing data about them. A search engine creates its own profile of a person. It can

> enable any internet user to obtain ... a structured overview of the information relating to that individual ... and which, without the search engine, could not have been interconnected or could have been only with great difficulty ...[4]

This potential interference with someone's data rights cannot be justified by 'merely the economic interest which the operator of such a search engine has in that processing'. The public did have an 'interest' in having information but, as a general rule, the rights of the 'data subject' override them.

Sr Costeja enjoyed a right, the court found, to ask a search engine to delist his information and his 'fundamental rights to the protection of those data and to privacy' encompassed a 'right to be forgotten'. Under certain conditions, the search engine was obliged to do as asked. An obligation to de-index 'may result' from the data being inaccurate but also if

> they are inadequate, irrelevant or excessive in relation to the purposes of the processing, that they are not kept up to date, or that they are kept for longer than necessary unless they are required to be kept for historical, statistical or scientific purposes.[5]

The judgment stressed that the complainant did not have to show that a link caused her or him 'prejudice' to succeed in having it delinked. A complainant's rights as a rule were superior to both the 'economic interest' of the search engine and 'the interest of the general public' in seeking information on that person. That might not be the case if the subject was in public life or if the public had a 'preponderant' interest in access to the information. How preponderance might be estimated was not specified.

No mention was made of the wider rights questions raised by either the Advocate-General or earlier court decisions (including those of the European Court of Human Rights) to which he had referred. It made repeatedly clear that, in data protection, the law's default assumption must be to prefer the information rights of the individual subject. The judgment treats search engines as economic, profit-seeking organisations without any reference to any public benefit they might provide. Search engines are private companies, but their techniques and services are also significant and useful to those seeking and circulating information. Reasoning which assumes that a company has only a single, profit-seeking function seems one-dimensional and unrealistic. Internet companies cannot be assumed to be operating solely in the public interest, however defined, but neither can the benefits they bring be ignored.

The issue of treating rights in tension with each other in a proportionate balance was barely mentioned and certainly not in the sense that the Advocate-General had framed it. Rights to know and freedom of expression are cursorily included. As one commentator put it, data protection had been elevated to a 'super-right'. That gave some help to the European Commission, whose officials were working slowly towards a revision of the law. One said that Google Spain 'clarified something about the status of search engines and it raised awareness. It prepared the ground for the new legislation. It was a wake-up call.'[6]

The judgment extended and consolidated data protection and privacy rights but left a number of issues either unconsidered or in a state of uncertainty:

- The reasoning about human rights is odd. The EU's Charter of Fundamental Rights is mentioned, but without mention of different rights which may compete or collide.
- There is no mention, even in disagreement, of parallel dilemmas judged by the European Court of Human Rights. In a 2013 case, the court rejected claims by two Polish lawyers who wanted newspaper articles, over which they had successfully sued for libel, removed from archives. Despite a strong basic case, the court judges warned that 'particularly strong reasons must be provided for any measure limiting access to information which the public has a right to receive' and was sceptical about 'rewriting history'.[7]
- The failure to consider freedom of expression is likely to set a precedent. In the words of one analysis:

> At a minimum, the CJEU [Court of Justice of the European Union] should have explicitly considered the search engine operator's right to freedom of expression and information, and should have given more

> *attention to people's right to receive and impart information. The CJEU suggests that 'as a rule', privacy and data protection rights override the public's interest in finding information. We fear that search engine operators, data protection authorities, and national courts might therefore not adequately consider the right to freedom of expression in their delisting decisions based on Google Spain.*[8]

- There is mention of balance but almost none of the linked idea of 'proportionality', which has featured heavily in previous court judgments in this area.
- Google Spain was technically a 'preliminary ruling' by the Court and it answers the questions put to it. The 'referring court' (in Spain) did not mention the right to freedom of expression. It is unclear, even to some experts, why 'rights' are being contrasted and compared to 'interests'. At two points the judgment appears to demote the public's right to access to information, guaranteed by Article 11 of the Charter of Fundamental Rights, to an 'interest'.[9]
- There is no acknowledgement even of the possibility that the usefulness or effectiveness of data protection law might be eroded by the speed and scale of technology change.
- The judgment contains little guidance for Google or any other search engine about the process which should be adopted to decide on delisting requests.
- The criteria for establishing a right to remove a link are open-ended and subjective. The fact that relevance, accuracy, and adequacy have been in the directive for years does not make them easy to adjudicate, particularly for a private-sector company. To take only one, an objective decision on whether a link is 'relevant' is an invitation to inconsistent standards. Relevant to whom or to what? Deciding relevance or adequacy would be hard to assess in a single culture. The coordination of agreement on this across 28 states is almost insoluble. Privacy, information rights, and free speech are ideas which vary even between apparently similar societies; procedural attempts at legal harmonisation do not necessarily change that.
- Two of the court's suggested criteria are dynamic. A linked fact about a person could be judged irrelevant at one moment and become relevant later. If Sr Costeja was ever to run for public office, a very thorough and conscientious journalist or researcher might find the reference to his debts and property auction in the archives at

La Vanguardia. But the public interest might lie in making that information more available in the context of his candidacy. As one expert on Google's Advisory Council asked, 'Who will act on behalf of the public interest in cases where information becomes relevant in the future?'[10]
- The court also said that facts which were accurate and properly reported originally may later fall into the category of those which can be obscured. How does a data protection authority or a court set the timetable for the expiry of a fact's significance? What happens if the significance alters?
- The definition of a 'public figure' raises the same kind of problems. Everyone can agree that an MP is a public figure. Is a CEO? Is a sports star? What scale of community or range of responsibilities qualify someone to be a public figure? Is a parish councillor? A priest? The chairman of a local chamber of commerce?
- Whatever process the court imagined for Google, it made no mention of whether the original publisher had any right to intervene in a delinking issue. The court did say that the directive does not oblige the search engine to notify the publisher of a delinking request. But do the author or publisher have any right to express an opinion on a move to, in the court's own words, consign their work to 'oblivion'?

The case was groundbreaking because it separated the rights of journalistic organisations (in this instance *La Vanguardia*) from search engines. The effect of the judgment may make some reporting harder because some information is taken out of search, but in the long term the work of journalists becomes more significant. Journalists supply and use archives which now contain some material to which the general public does not have easy access through a search engine.

The court had attempted a compromise: links could be removed under certain conditions but the original texts remained accessible and unchanged. The heads of EU data protection authorities met over the months after the judgment to examine some of the questions above and to try to provide guidance. Similarly, a number of national courts found themselves deciding issues on de-indexing requests which had been refused. But they were attempting to interpret a judgment which left information rights confused and the reach of the newly prominent right to be forgotten uncertain. Sr Costeja had become unforgettable.

5

Reactions and Consequences

A local difficulty triggered a worldwide debate. The Google Spain judgment, whatever may happen to its main findings in the future, achieved three things. First, it directed attention to a previously neglected area of increasing importance. The court at least highlighted the difficulty of determining what we do about internet content which may cause indefensible harm. Second, the judgment delivered a quick, simple way for people to correct uncontroversial mistakes. We still don't know exactly what proportion of requests that might be, but it seems fair to assume that some, probably many, pose no problem of any kind. People know where to go to request delinking; the process is relatively fast and cheap. Third, the judgment brought Google within the scope of the law. The judgment might have been unbalanced and the law may not work well, but that is not the same as saying that Google has no responsibility for its links. Since the judgment, Google executives have implicitly acknowledged that it should have acted earlier on some complaints.[1]

Reaction to the court's decision was immediate and criticism dominated the headlines. Google called the decision 'disappointing' but its representatives were careful to stress that the company would comply. Jimmy Wales, the founder of Wikipedia, called it a 'deep injustice and terrible danger in European law', adding:

> *I think the decision will have no impact on people's right to privacy, because I don't regard truthful information in court records published by court order in a newspaper to be private information. If anything, the decision is likely to simply muddle the interesting philosophical questions and make it more difficult to make real progress on privacy issues. In the case of truthful, non-defamatory information obtained legally, I think there is no possibility of any defensible 'right' to censor what other people are saying. It is important to avoid language like 'data' because we aren't talking about 'data' — we are talking about the suppression of knowledge.*[2]

Ashley Hurst, a London lawyer specialising in information law, took aim at the language: 'For a landmark judgment, it is hard to imagine a more opaque set of guiding principles.'[3] Geoff King of the US-based Committee to Protect Journalists thought that the parallels with Orwell were exaggerated but managed to quote the author nevertheless:

> By robbing journalists and other researchers of context, and the public of its right to know, the European Court's ruling portends an uncertain period for press freedom and rational thought. And while the use of 'Orwellian' may be overwrought, given the Court's laudable aims, the author's warning nonetheless still echoes: 'Who controls the past controls the future; who controls the present controls the past.'[4]

More than one expert commentator with some knowledge of the case's background suspected Google of orchestrating furious reactions while trying to make sure that the company's fingerprints were nowhere to be seen. Julia Powles was having none of it:

> The whole 'this opens the way for repressive governments to censor the internet' is a complete scare tactic, completely disconnected from the facts of the case. It's an easy and lazy argument with pernicious consequences, because it's part of the broader anti-regulation narrative of the internet behemoths.[5]

European Commissioner Reding saw no clash of rights at all:

> The right to be forgotten and the right to free information are not foes but friends. ... It's not about protecting one at the expense of the other but striking the right balance in order to protect both. The European Court made it clear that two rights do not make a wrong and has given clear directions on how this balance can be found and where the limits of the right to be forgotten lie. The Court also made clear that journalistic work must not be touched; it is to be protected.[6]

One English academic expert, Paul Bernal, argued that freedom of information had gained:

> It's had a positive impact on freedom of information. Most people don't go past the first page of search results. If you delist something, other things come up. The 'speech rights' of people lower down the list have been

enhanced and access to information improved. Power users of search will find stuff. Casual users won't if it is slightly less accessible. All this applies, of course, if the judgment is implemented correctly.[7]

A House of Lords committee issued a rapid report which pointed out that technology developments rendered much of data protection law unfeasible. Individuals had been offered an 'uncontested' right of censorship. The report's claim that the ruling would be 'unworkable' was undermined, at least in the short term, by the relatively smooth process which Google rolled out for request-handling. The Lords recommended that the EU data protection regulation in preparation should reverse the court decision by removing a right to be forgotten or to erasure. There was no sign in Brussels of anyone intending to do anything of the sort. The (then) Culture Secretary in Britain's coalition government, Sajid Javid, gave a speech to newspaper editors condemning 'Luxembourg's unelected judges' for restricting media freedom and ordering censorship by the back door. Mr Javid was apparently unaware that colleagues from a different government department had for several years been negotiating the fine print of a new regulation incorporating a right to be forgotten.

Within a few weeks of the judgment, Google posted a simple web form with which delinking requests could be made.[8] Officials at the European Commission wanted and expected Google to use a law firm to process the delinking requests which the judgment allowed. Google hired a group of paralegals[9] and kept the process in-house. It was not as if the company had no experience of editing what appeared in search. By the beginning of 2016, the company was receiving and processing 70 million copyright removal requests a month, a figure which puts the right to be forgotten procedures in the shade. In the second half of 2014, it dealt with just over 3,500 government requests to take down material. Sensitive private information such as passport details, bank account numbers, or personal medical data are also routinely delinked. As of mid-2015, Google has also made available a web form for requesting the removal of 'revenge porn', a further belated acknowledgement of social, civic responsibilities.[10]

The requests to have links removed came in considerable volume: around 40,000 requests arrived in the first two days. The legal climate was changed by the decision. Max Mosley, the Formula One boss who had featured in the *News of the World* under the unforgettable headline 'F1 Boss has Sick Nazi Orgy with Five Hookers', had taken legal action in France and Germany to force search engines to restrict access to the photographs which had accompanied the story. Google had been fighting the cases but now backed down, conceding that it had the technical means to block access to certain pictures while leaving the rest of the story alone. Google also settled the case of Daniel Hegglin, a businessman living in Hong Kong who had been the subject of a prolonged campaign of online harassment and trolling. He had sued Google for not doing enough about it. Google undertook to make unspecified but 'significant' efforts to police the material by taking down links.

Media and information rights lawyers who had been living for 20 years with the Data Protection Act in the UK began, as result of Google Spain, to see greater possibilities in the neglected law because of its wide potential use and narrow afterthought defences for free speech. A minatory letter from a celebrated firm of London solicitors arrived at the offices of *Private Eye* in 2016 warning the magazine about risks of reporting on past links between animal rights extremists and John Beggs, himself now a prominent lawyer. Since the magazine last mentioned Beggs, the letter said, privacy law has been tightened – not least by the right to be forgotten.[11]

In 2015, for example, the much-reported celebrities Ashton Kutcher and Mila Kunis sued Mail Online over pictures of them with their baby daughter. The legal action was double-barrelled: they alleged breach of privacy and of data protection. Mail Online regularly runs alongside its extensive celebrity coverage panels which offer users the chance to buy clothes (or versions of them) worn in photographs appearing on the site. 'Go grey like Ashton in his slick sweater' said Mail Online's 'female fashion finder' next to the story about Kutcher and Kunis, which also carried an offer for an item of Kunis's clothing. Kutcher and Kunis's lawyers not only based a damages claim on privacy violation but also on the grounds that the clothing advertisement processed personal data without permission. The case has not been heard at the time of writing, but the targeting of the advertisement suggests that the celebrities' lawyers calculate that the publisher might have a defence under the Data Protection Act for 'journalism' but none for an advertisement. Did the framers of EU and national law imagine it as a weapon in the armoury of celebrity public relations?

Google's new powers

Google Spain may have been a defeat in court for Google but it gave the search engine a new power of decision. Those choices were open to challenge: a dissatisfied complainant who is refused delisting can appeal to the local data protection authority (in the UK the Information Commissioner's Office) and, if still not satisfied and equipped with patience and money, can ask a court to review. One informal estimate made from regulators' statistics found that less than 1 per cent of Google decisions were challenged by being referred to them.

The court had given no guidance about how delisting requests should be handled. A pan-European panel of experts was set up by Google and held public hearings in major European cities.[12] The advisers made only two recommendations which disagree with the data protection authorities.[13] They advised Google to notify the publishers and platforms concerned that links had been taken down. They disagreed with the majority of data protection authorities in finding that the breaking of links should be confined to EU domains and that links should remain in the rest of the world. So for 18 months after the judgment a link which did not appear in google.co.uk remained live on google.com. Then, in a concession designed to influence a battle with the French data protection authority, Google stopped the workaround, preventing name searches from European domains being directed at google.com.

Commentators asked if these were decisions which ought to be made by a private sector company at all. In the view of Professor Luciano Floridi, who chaired Google's advisory council on the issue in 2014, 'It's a half-baked solution. If Europe really wanted to regain control over personal data, giving Google this type of power is an odd outcome.'[14] Google itself admits to some doubt when explaining the implications of the case to its users: 'These are difficult judgements and as a private organization, we may not be in a good position to decide on your case. If you disagree with our decision you can contact your local DPA [Data Protection Authority].'[15]

Indeed, Google implicitly acknowledged that the court had raised an important question which, whatever the disagreements over how exactly it ought to be answered, Google had neglected. Google's chief legal counsel David Drummond said that

> it's hard not to empathise with some of the requests that we've seen – from the man who asked that we do not show a news article saying that he had been questioned in connection with a crime (he's able to demonstrate that he was never charged) to the mother who requested that we remove news articles for her daughter's name as she had been the victim of abuse.[16]

Why should private-sector companies be as thorough about this as a court might be? Google, accused by the EU's powerful competition lawyers of abusing a dominant market position, certainly had a strong corporate motive to cooperate willingly and quickly. But it also has the leverage and resources not to roll over, and can fight to the finish any dispute which it cares to take the distance. But would that apply to all search engines which might be the target of such judgments (given that it is unclear precisely which ones might be affected)?

In all likelihood, the search engine companies will remain the first place that a delinking request can be evaluated. Budgets differ from state to state, but no data protection authority is richly provided for. One researcher calculated that the average annual budget of EU authorities is €3.5m and that somewhere between a quarter and a half never take any enforcement action; all deal with a wide range of issues and disputes under the law well beyond complaints about search engines.[17]

Experts in smaller countries quickly pointed out that smaller search engines might have obvious capacity problems with imitating Google's evaluation procedure. 'Are mini-competitors of Google like seznam.cz also capable of doing this? I doubt so. They will most likely just automate the process to save costs.'[18] In the short run, small search engines seemed unlikely to face these demands as the court judgment lays stress on Google's size and market share, implying that delinking obligations might not be automatically imposed on smaller equivalents. So far, the other search engines to set up a systematic approach have been Bing and Yahoo.[19]

The advantages of Google's process lie in its simplicity and speed. But a company is not a neutral arbiter as a court or civic institution is positioned to be. Courts operate on the default assumption that justice should be seen to be done unless there are compelling reasons to the contrary; a company is under no such obligation. But it is unlikely that a data protection authority in even the larger states could have coped with the flow of requests. Several months after Google had set up its system, the EU's national data protection authorities issued guidance about the handling of requests. The list of tests for deciding delisting[20] is slightly different from the accounts given by Google[21] but there is only one major disagreement, over the geographic reach of delinking. But the list from the 'Article 29 Working Party' is advice only. Google is not formally obliged to comply in detail nor obliged to release information about how these decisions are being made.

A number of rights are in play when a piece of information might be obscured. De-indexing an item from a search engine – even if the original publication still exists – may affect the rights of the ordinary consumer of information, whose right to 'receive and impart information and ideas' is guaranteed by the EU's charter. It may also affect the exercise of free expression rights by either the author or the publisher.

Google currently notifies a webmaster (who is registered with it) when a link has been broken, although the data protection authorities would prefer that it did not do this routinely and stress that publishers have no legal right to know this.[22] But there is no procedure for anyone who might disagree with a delisting decision to challenge it: the system is not adversarial and there is no hearing unless or until a case reaches a court. A publisher made aware that a link has been broken does not know who has asked for this, still less the reasons which have been given. Google keeps records of broad categories of refused requests but does not record any data on why a delisting is accepted.

We know something about what types of material people want delisted. Six days after the court ruling, before the review process had been established and with only a few thousand requests, Google issued figures which showed that 12 per cent of the delisting requests concerned child pornography, 20 per cent serious or violent crime, and 31 per cent fraud or scams.[23] No further breakdown of such categories has since been provided and it's likely that this is because, as the number of requests grew, later results turned out to be less dramatic. The platform which is the subject of the largest number of delinking requests is Facebook. By May 2016, some 13,000 Facebook links had been removed from view. The eight sites for which Google receives the most requests are either social media or profiling sites.

Source code in Google's 'Transparency Report' revealed a different picture, analysing 220,000 requests made before spring 2015. The data, covering more than three-quarters of the requests to that point, showed that fewer than 5 per cent of requests were from criminals, politicians, or high-profile public figures. Around half of requests which Google had classed as 'private/personal' had been granted; the success rate for requests in 'political', 'crime', 'child protection', or 'public figure' had been between 17 per cent and 22 per cent. Google acknowledged the data but said that the analysis had been stopped because the results were not reliable enough for publication.[24]

The researchers who found these data argued that Google had, by keeping the figures under wraps and discreetly encouraging protests about controversial instances of delinking, distorted what was happening to bolster their case against the right to be forgotten. Google may well have been doing that, but rights questions do not turn on percentages. It may well be that the large majority of requests received and decided by Google do not raise any significant public interest issue. That would not prevent a small percentage in single figures containing a handful of stories which should remain retrievable and linked in the public interest. Scale is not the only measure of importance.

Google has disclosed three limited types of information: overall numbers of requests and URLs delisted,[25] a few heavily edited examples, and some descriptions of their decision-making criteria, usually delivered on an off-the-record basis at specialist seminars. Three examples:

> *After we removed a news story about a minor crime, the newspaper published a story about the removal action. The Information Commissioner's Office ordered us to remove the second story from search results for the individual's name. We removed the page from search results for the individual's name. (UK)*
>
> *A high-ranking public official asked us to remove recent articles discussing a decades-old criminal conviction. We did not remove the articles from search results. (Hungary)*
>
> *A teacher convicted for a minor crime over 10 years ago asked us to remove an article about the conviction. We have removed the pages from search results for the individual's name. (Germany)*

These thumbnail sketches disclose nothing about what matters most in such choices. What exactly is being weighed? How and by whom? On what does the decision turn? How are rights which compete being weighed? Google provides plenty of detail about process but very little about substance.

There is no reason to suppose that Google staff or advisers are not doing this carefully and thoroughly. But quasi-legal decisions are normally taken by a process which is accountable partly because it is visible. The phrase 'open court' refers to the ability of anyone to inspect proceedings. Deciding what information to remove or obscure in the public sphere need not necessarily involve the panoply of a judge, jury, and lawyers. We are still a very long way from being in a position to evaluate what is happening as the world's most powerful search engine edits its results.

This is a (lightly edited) version of what Google tells us about the reasons why its team might delist:

- 'Clear absence of public interest': For example, aggregator sites with pages that contain personal contact or address information, instances where the requester's name no longer appears on the page, and pages that are no longer online (404 error).

- Sensitive information: Pages with content that relates solely to information about someone's health, sexual orientation, race, ethnicity, religion, political affiliation, and trade-union status.
- Content relating to minors: Content that relates to minors or to minor crimes that occurred when the requester was a minor.
- Spent convictions/exonerations/acquittals for crimes: Consistent with local law governing the rehabilitation of offenders, they tend to weigh in favour of delisting content relating to a conviction that is spent, accusations that are proven false in a court of law, or content relating to a criminal charge of which the requester was acquitted.

Some of the most common material factors involved in decisions not to delist pages are:

- Alternative solutions: There's another avenue for the requestor to delist that page from the search results.
- Technical reasons: An incomplete or broken URL is a common technical error.
- Duplicate URL by same individual: A requester submits multiple requests to delist the same page for the same name.
- Strong public interest: 'We may decline to delist if we determined that the page contains information which is strongly in the public interest. Determining whether content is in the public interest is complex and may mean considering many diverse factors, including – but not limited to – whether the content relates to the requester's professional life, a past crime, political office, position in public life, or whether the content itself is self-authored content, government documents, or journalistic in nature.'[26]

A group of academics addressed an open appeal to Google for more detailed information that need not compromise individual privacy. The signatories[27] said that data protection authorities 'seemed content' to be reassured by the fact that appeal rates were low, but that is hardly enough:

> The vast majority of these decisions face no public scrutiny, though they shape public discourse. What's more, the values at work in this process will/should inform information policy around the world. A fact-free debate about the RTBF [right to be forgotten] is in no one's interest.
> ... Peter Fleischer, Google global privacy counsel, reportedly ... [said] 'Over time, we are building a rich program of jurisprudence on the [RTBF] decision.' ... It is a jurisprudence built in the dark.[28]

Public commentary by Google's legal team has not added much to this. William Malcolm, a counsel in London, has said that a 'reputable and recent' news story is unlikely to be delisted. He also said that they had seen a small number of cases by very public figures attempting, unsuccessfully, to delist content they do not like.[29] Other sources indicate that the definition of public figures is broad: someone recognised at national or international level. They include business people and celebrities. This is mostly done by a search of relevant URLs or names. The question of what to do with criteria which might change over time (a profile which changes from private to public) has not been tackled. Around one in six requests are aimed at journalistic content and a large majority are rejected.[30]

A fraction of these judgement calls have trickled into the light. A few requests reaching Google emerge from the disputes that reach open court, taken there by a complainant determined and affluent enough to take the dispute to a third stage after a request has been denied by both the search engine and by the data protection authority.

Cases which have surfaced

The case of Malcolm Edwards revealed that not all applicants for Google's sympathy deserve it. Edwards, a former law lecturer and lay preacher who previously called himself Edwards-Sayer, pleaded guilty in 2007 to eight counts of conspiring to cheat the public revenue. For his role in a £51m VAT fraud, he was sentenced to six-and-a-half years. Out of prison on licence towards the end of his sentence, Edwards sued several news organisations to have reports of his crime removed on the grounds that his actions were history, having been committed a decade before. The length of his sentence meant that his offences would not be 'spent' under the Rehabilitation of Offenders Act. The news organisations, which included the BBC, the *Guardian*, and the *Nottingham Evening Post*, argued that it was in the public interest for the reports to remain available. Edwards then sued Google, relying on arguments from the Google Spain case. His application was dismissed by a judge who said that it was 'totally without merit'.[31]

In December 2014, the French High Court ordered Google to remove a link to the online archive of the *Le Parisien* newspaper from 2006. This reported the conviction of a Madame X for fraud and a prison sentence of three years. This item was near the top of a Google search for her name in 2014. The court took the view that eight years was long enough for the trial report to be out of date and that the new right to de-index the link overrode Google's counter-claim that it should be retained in the public interest.

Of the first five links to material published by the *New York Times* which Google told the paper had been delisted, two were marriage announcements and one a death notice. Another was a report from 2002 about a decision by a US court to close three websites that the federal government accused of selling an estimated $1m worth of unusable web addresses. The original report named three British companies and two men from London who controlled them. The fifth delisting was a mystery: a feature on an acrobatic show called 'Villa Villa' which hoped 'to get a generation raised on MTV interested in seeing live theater'.[32] The BBC was notified in May 2015 of the delisting of a short report on a car crash which named no individual.[33]

The BBC keeps an online list of URLs linking to its reporting which have been de-indexed.[34] In the view of BBC News Online's Managing Editor Neil McIntosh, the majority of delistings from the BBC site are reports of court cases or pre-trial coverage. Online search can summon any fragment of an arrest, charge, or trial and so risk a piece of information being read out of context (someone charged, for example, with an offence of which they were later acquitted). So it is not surprising that requests may focus on what people perceive as harm and that some campaigners feel that the 'Google effect' undermines the Rehabilitation of Offenders Act.[35] But it is also possible that the right to be forgotten could cut cross the rules of that Act and alter its operation in practice if search engines do not follow it when processing requests from complainants.

English judges seem reluctant to reopen cases in which the Information Commissioner's Office has refused to back an individual whose delinking request has been refused by Google. In July 2015, the Administrative Court turned down an application from a Mr Kashaba for judicial review of an ICO decision that he had no grounds for URLs being taken down. He had asked for the de-indexing of articles which apparently revealed that Mr Khashaba had failed in his legal attempts to get his gun licences reinstated and had also failed to obtain placement on the Register of Medical Specialists in Ireland. The judge told Mr Kashaba that if he wanted to take the matter further, he would have to sue Google.[36]

Google's delisting decisions have not provoked a large number of appeals to data protection authorities or courts. The notifications contain no details. By early 2016, Finland's ombudsman was handling 31 appeals arising from 2,035 rejections (a rate of 1.5 per cent). The first decision to come before the ombudsman revealed a broad meaning for a 'public figure'. The ombudsman said that Google did not have to delist links about a businessman because the business register 'lists the man as still being involved in business operations, including debt collection'.

One of the earliest judgments which attempted to contain the potentially wide scope of the right to be forgotten was made in an Amsterdam court in September 2014. The complainant was an escort agency owner sentenced to six years in prison in 2012 for 'attempted incitement of contract killing'. The intended victim, whose murder the agency owner was filmed discussing, was a competitor in what the court coyly referred to as 'the escort sector'. Google had agreed to delink some URLs but refused others. The Dutch judge made quite clear that he interpreted the rights established by Google Spain narrowly and that there are other rights to be considered.

> *The [Google Spain] judgment does not intend to protect individuals against all negative communications on the Internet, but only against 'being pursued' for a long time by 'irrelevant', 'excessive' or 'unnecessarily defamatory' expressions.*

In fact the judges in Google Spain had not drawn the right to be forgotten as precisely as that. The Amsterdam judges argued for a common-sense view of what would usually be remembered about a serious crime and can legitimately be kept on the record:

> *The conviction for a serious crime such as the one at issue and the negative publicity as a consequence thereof, in general provide information about an individual that will remain relevant. The negative qualifications that may be involved will only be 'excessive' or 'unnecessarily defamatory' in very exceptional cases, for instance when the offense committed is brought up again without a clear reason, apparently for no other purpose than to damage the individual involved, if reporting is not factual but rather a 'slanging-match'.*[37]

Another Dutch case was a rare example of legal action reversing a Google delisting. It also acted as a reminder that no one can be forced to forget something and a person may exercise a right to remind society of a fact that someone else might want forgotten. (The case also served as an oblique reminder that a crime cannot be forgiven without being known.) A convicted murderer had successfully requested Google to delink search results featuring his name. The father of one of his victims discovered this and published news of it on the website of the Dutch Federation of Surviving Relatives of Violent Crime. The convict sued, using the Google Spain precedent, to have that article delisted. The court took note that the crime was only ten years old and declined to stop the new publicity about the crime:

> *The conviction for a serious offence goes hand in hand with negative publicity; such publicity is in general permanently relevant to the person of the convict. However, the opposite right to be forgotten as a perpetrator of a serious crime becomes more weighty as the event lies further back in time, and the perpetrator has further redeemed his 'debt' to society in general and to the surviving relatives in particular.*[38]

A third Dutch case involving a KPMG partner began before Google Spain but one party to the case hoped to use the judgment when it came. The KPMG partner was entangled in a dispute with a builder of a new house he had commissioned. At one point, the builder changed the locks on the new house, forcing his client to seek shelter as best he could. The Dutch daily *De Telegraaf* ran a front-page story in 2012 headlined 'KPMG Top Executive Camps in Container'. Google refused to take down links to the story in 2014; the KPMG partner sued, invoking Google Spain. Many people he met mentioned the story to him, he said; it harmed his work since new clients searched for the story. The information was irrelevant because two-and-a-half years old. He also asked the court to delete the footnote which appears at the foot of all Google searches in European domains for individual names ('Some results may have been removed under data protection law in Europe') when his name was entered.

The court went to some lengths to try to put delinking in context. Search engines play an important role. Subject them to too many restrictions and they would not function so well. Two fundamental rights were at stake: privacy and freedom of information. Data protection law was not aimed at hiding lawful publications. The court refused the KPMG partner's claim.

Not all attempts to delist went smoothly. In 2010, a Scottish football referee Dougie McDonald was involved in a row over a penalty at a Celtic match when he subsequently admitted to lying to the Celtic manager about the reasons for awarding the penalty. McDonald retired as a referee after the controversy. In the early weeks of de-indexing, three links to this episode as reported in the *Guardian* and two to the *Daily Telegraph* were removed. Google later reversed both these decisions when both papers repeated a summary of the story when drawing attention to the deletions.

But even if those links had stayed broken, the degree of obscurity someone (presumably Mr McDonald) had obtained was small. Quite apart from the fact that both newspapers retained their articles online, a search on his name was not the only route to finding out why Mr McDonald had retired so suddenly. Anyone searching for 'Scottish referee who lied' would find the articles immediately. Until late 2015 when Google blocked this workaround, anyone searching for 'Dougie McDonald' on google.com from Europe would also have found the reports whose links had been taken down in Google's European domains. 'If this is brand management,' the *Guardian*'s head of search engine optimisation Chris Moran wrote, 'it's a very leaky form of it.' A study led by New York University looked at 283 news articles publicly identified as delisted and looked at how easy it would be to 'rediscover' the articles and identify who had made the request. They estimated that anyone with undergraduate-level computer science skills could find 30–40 per cent of the material.[39]

The 'Streisand effect'

The objections to the creation of a right to be forgotten were strong enough to provoke what privacy lawyers call, after the singer, the 'Streisand effect'. Complaining about any breach of personal privacy almost invariably risks a repetition or aggravation of the original disclosure. The *Daily Telegraph* and *Daily Mail* have regularly reported links to their own stories which have been taken down. The gay news website *Pink News* has published a list of 19 stories delinked, claiming that this is 'infringement of press freedom'. The stories include allegations of homophobic comments by a BBC star and a report about a gay porn actor trying to smuggle crystal meth on to a transatlantic flight to the UK.

Google Spain did cause a switch in tactics by law firms: injured parties no longer needed to calculate the risks of ponderous and expensive litigation. Richer complainants still had advantages but the opportunity of redress was spread wider. Dan Tench, an experienced media lawyer at the London partnership Olswang, said that a combination of the reforms to libel law in 2013 (which had the effect of making successful claims harder) and the Google Spain case had changed the nature of his work. 'I just do much less defamation and privacy work now. In many cases, clients see the right to be forgotten as the quick, easy route to go.'

Law firms with media or information rights practices were not slow to see that, even if Google had tried to make requests simple and do-it-yourself, there was a potential market for advice and help. Put 'right to be forgotten solicitors' into Google in the UK and the second link which came up in early 2016 was headed: 'Right To Be Forgotten – Get Results Removed' from Brett Wilson LLP, whose question-and-answer at the linked page does explain that the right is not absolute and the tests which need to be passed for removal. It adds:

> We have submitted requests to Google on behalf of senior executives of multinationals and PLCs, celebrities, models, lawyers, teachers, pilots and those involved in business and the arts. Our efforts have led to the successful removal of links that include information relating to past/spent convictions, disciplinary sanctions, offensive blog articles, news reports, private/intimate images, workplace investigations and employment disputes.[40]

You do not need to be a lawyer to offer reputation help. Bertrand Girin, a French venture capital and pharmaceutical executive, had begun an advisory service Reputation VIP in 2009, based in Lyon. In the wake of Google Spain, that site quickly began another simply called forget.me. Of 1,106 requests processed in the site's first week, the largest category was people asking for their home address to be de-indexed. The next largest were 'negative opinions', 'redundancy', and 'origin, nationality or ethnic identity'. No interest is evident in either the truth of what appeared or any possible public interest in knowing what was recorded. The ill-defined wording of the tests for delisting set out in Google Spain has allowed the obscuring of information which does not belong in the public domain, some which might lie on a disputed borderline, and some which ought to be retrievable in the public interest. It cannot be in the public interest for these distinctions to be so easily elided.

Guidelines

The European Court never elaborates on its own judgments but the data protection authorities, assembled as the Article 29 Working Party, did so six months after the decision. The document they produced makes an attempt to clarify the judgment but, unable to contradict the judges, cannot untangle the largest problems or undo the tunnel vision approach of data protection law.

The guidelines nod towards the need for balance. But they follow the court's distinction between the *rights* to data protection and privacy and the public's *interest* in knowing, leaving unstated the clear implication that a right outranks an interest. The furthest they can go in encouraging balance is to say that 'if the interest of the public overrides the rights of the data subject, delisting will not be appropriate'.[41] The issue of which search engines may be affected is left wide open: 'The ruling is specifically addressed to generalist search engines, but that does not mean that it cannot be applied to other intermediaries', adding that as a rule it should not apply to search engines 'with a restricted field of action' such as newspaper website searches.

The detailed section on criteria for delisting decisions does something which the European Court did not do: it cites European Court of Human Rights judgments on distinguishing between private and public figures, including this:

> *A fundamental distinction needs to be made between reporting facts capable of contributing to a debate in a democratic society, relating to politicians in the exercise of their official functions for example, and reporting details of the private life of an individual who does not exercise such functions.*[42]

This distinction may sound clear on the face of it, but the questions which it begs are at the centre of a case briefly in the UK courts in 2014, which is an example of the new attempts to use data protection law against journalists. Global Witness, an NGO which monitors corruption around the world, reported first in 2012 that the mining company BSG Resources Ltd had won a concession to mine iron ore in Guinea by paying bribes. Four executives who work for or had worked for BSG sued, not for libel but alleging that their personal data had been 'processed' illegally by Global Witness. At the first stage of the case, a court sent one of the issues before it to the Information Commissioner's Office. The ICO ruled that campaigning journalism was still journalism and data processed by journalists was thus protected from action under Section 32 of the Data Protection Act.

The case went quiet and the ICO judgment seems reasonable, not least because the Commissioner took a broad view of the 'journalism' exemption. In general, the ICO's defence of free expression has been thorough and conscientious. That assessment might not apply throughout the rest of Europe. Suppose that the exemption for 'journalistic' work had been held not to apply or that a court overruled the ICO. Would all courts have held that the BSG executives were 'public figures'? They may have been involved in an issue which should be known and debated, but the claimants would likely have argued that they were private individuals.

The Article 29 Working Party's guidelines give a number of questions and answers which attempt to clarify the tests for de-indexing a link about a person. Is the data accurate? Is the data subject a minor? Is the data processing causing prejudice to the subject? Two of the vaguest criteria are 'relevance' and the age of the data in dispute. The guidelines point out that they are closely connected. But on age, the question is left open for data protection authorities and courts to interpret: 'Depending on the facts of the case, information that was published a long time ago, e.g. 15 years ago, might be less relevant than information published 1 year ago.' No guidance is offered on information dated between those two points.

Google has been notifying most webmasters when a link is taken down. The regulators came out against this:

> Search engine managers should not as a general practice inform the webmasters of the pages affected by de-listing of the fact that some webpages cannot be acceded from the search engine in response to specific queries. Such a communication has no legal basis under EU data protection law.

It concedes only that it may be legitimate for search engines to contact webmasters to get a 'fuller understanding' of a case. If there is any aspect of Google Spain and its consequences which deserves to be challenged at some time in the future it is this. Such an interpretation of the judgment effectively removes any chance of any adversarial process which might weigh the rights in conflict – and it does so because that balance is expressly excluded by the EU's data protection law. Several individuals or groups might object to a delisting which makes information hard to find: the original publisher, the author, or any members of the public who might wish to argue that this is information which should not be obscured. If there is no obligation to notify, no process to take account of these claims can even begin. Google has attempted to negotiate arrangements with publishers for their involvement 'pre-decision' on delisting requests, but agreement has not been reached. If a news media organisation takes a 'strategic' case through the courts (and perhaps to the European Court of Human Rights rather than to the European Court of Justice) it is most likely to turn on the issue of access and process for all parties who claim a right to intervene in a decision to delist.

The most controversial advice given by the data protection authorities was over the geography of the right to be forgotten. Google, they said, was wrong to restrict takedowns to internet domains in the EU: a link which had been available anywhere and removed should disappear everywhere. EU law should not be circumvented. This dispute is largely beyond the scope of this study because it raises the wide question known to lawyers as 'extra-territoriality' and because it is still being negotiated as this study goes to press. Can a law be enforced outside the jurisdiction in which it operates? The French data protection authority has issued notice to Google that it must take down links outside Europe. Critics of this approach say that this will encourage the unscrupulous to use a Europe-based complaint to have embarrassing links rendered invisible outside the EU. Google has made several concessions to the French ruling but not so far complied fully and could face large fines if no settlement is reached.[43]

The aftermath of the Google Spain judgment did not fulfil the predictions of an immediate disaster for freedom of expression or 'censorship'. Many small injustices have been righted; a wide-ranging discussion on the value of digital communication began. But the judgment also sowed the seeds of trouble. Most law is framed to balance precision with flexibility in the face of circumstances. Much good law is broad and even sometimes vague. It comes into focus as precedents and judgments accumulate. Some judgments after Google Spain have supported the right to know. Others have limited it. They have not helped to define a precise remedy to a specific problem.

6

Beyond Europe

Anxieties over the potential harm which can be wrought by the accumulative, ineradicable nature of data retention and retrieval are not confined to Europe. With some of the strongest legal protections of personal data in the world, the EU is naturally influential. This chapter explores both parallel developments on rights to be forgotten outside Europe and the global impact of Google Spain.

Lines of distinction about what can or should be disclosed in a given society is both a delicate compromise and one which has taken years, and most probably centuries, to evolve and be iterated by public debate. Harmonising the data protection laws of the 28 states of the EU has thrown up numerous problems. Attempting it for the world is truly optimistic. But, defenders of data protection insist, digital technology is almost borderless and rules will not be respected and enforceable unless they can cross borders with the ease that bits of information travel.

In 2015, the Italian parliament decided that its contribution to entrenching fundamental rights on the internet throughout the world would be a Declaration of Internet Rights. Given that one-third of Italians have not yet used the internet (one of the highest such proportions in the EU),[1] it is an unexpected place for this movement to start. The language of rights is always general and idealistic, but even by the standards of such documents, the text[2] agreed by the MPs in Rome is hard to connect with the way in which digital life is being lived now. The declaration also catches the widespread sense that something of this kind is needed. But a strong feeling is not always a good basis for law.

The section on personal data in the Italian Declaration includes these assertions:

> *Data must be processed in accordance with the principles of necessity, purpose limitation, relevance, proportionality and, in any case, the right of every individual to informational self-determination shall prevail ...*

> Consent does not constitute a legal basis for the processing of data when there is a significant imbalance of power between the data subject and the data processor.

Leaving aside the questions of global enforcement, which are neither small nor resolved, the first of these clauses uses tests which are familiar to Italian and EU data protection law. But they may be harder to define in non-European cultures and languages; they also rely on subjective interpretation. The second clause above would, if taken literally, invalidate almost every consent agreement which is signed or ticked at an internet site. It would be hard for any internet user to identify a site to which they had given implicit or explicit consent which was not more powerful than an individual, however that power might be measured.

Although the Declaration contains wording which acknowledges the importance of freedom of speech and the right to know, it reproduces the imbalance of EU data protection law by treating these knowledge rights not as something to be held in delicate balance with privacy and data protection but as subsidiary qualifications and exemptions.

Israel, Asia, New Zealand, Australia

Google has found itself arguing that it should not act as a censor in many different jurisdictions. In Israel, a lawyer brought proceedings to have a link taken down for a page which referred to a client of his under the headline 'Lawyer convicted in five different cases'. The court observed that the headline had been written by a website which routinely recorded such cases and accepted Google's argument that it was being asked to act as 'super-censor'. 'Google', the judgment said, 'cannot be unconditionally directed to remove search results any time a person asks them to take down something they don't like.'[3]

The idea of a right to be forgotten, although aired and debated long before Google Spain, was propelled around the world by surprise at the case's outcome. In advance of a conference of privacy authorities in Asia which happened to take place weeks after the European Court spoke, Hong Kong's privacy commissioner said that he was asking Google to extend the same request and takedown evaluation process to Hong Kong in imitation of the European procedure. He acknowledged that he did not expect it to be backed by law but hoped that Google would cooperate anyway.

Commissioner Allan Chiang Yam-wang clearly had been influenced by the court in Luxembourg:

> As a responsible enterprise, Google should also entertain removal requests from other parts of the world to meet their privacy expectations. We are not exercising a legal right but requesting a service that is available to EU citizens.[4]

The English-speaking press in Hong Kong did not agree. The *South China Morning Post*'s columnist Alex Lo pivoted his argument on the risk of de-indexing material which was true:

> We must not follow a terribly bad decision made by a foreign court just because Chiang thinks it's a good idea. ... Note that we are not talking about links to public records that are libellous, false or in violation of copyrights or intellectual property, but those that are perfectly legitimate and accurate.
>
> 'Online discussion has a pivotal role in Hong Kong's freedom of expression,' said Claudia Mo, a lawmaker on the territory's legislative council. 'The people's right to know should override the individual's right to be forgotten ... To make a law to eradicate history is something else.'[5]

But the Asia-Pacific debate on privacy, given new impetus by the news from Europe, took a different tack and tone from the start. As elsewhere, the privacy or data protection authorities certainly saw a problem which needed attention and they analysed Google Spain in detail. But there was markedly less enthusiasm for swinging the law into immediate action in a sensitive area where conflicting rights can't easily be reconciled. They were also more realistic about what can actually be forgotten.

John Edwards, New Zealand's privacy commissioner, asked the public for their reactions in a blogpost, warning that the phrase which started it all is misleading: 'I'm not a big fan of the term "right to be forgotten" for a number of reasons. It is inaccurate, imprecise and impossible – these being the three main ones.' Edwards was not unsympathetic to the idea that some privacy claims might obscure or erase private information that was true – but in clearly limited and defined circumstances closely overseen by regulators or courts. The American courts had created the idea of 'practical obscurity' in the 1980s, not allowing erasure of information but allowing it to be made harder to find. That idea was picked up in 1986 New Zealand high court case in which the judge said that privacy could 'grow back' over facts that were no longer relevant. In 1999, an eminent Australian jurist had presciently analysed early search engines such as Alta Vista and predicted the rise of demand for 'a right not to be indexed'.

But Edwards also reminded his readers that if a 'right to be forgotten case' came before him, he would be following New Zealand's privacy act which tells him to work for

> *the protection of important human rights and social interests that compete with privacy, including the general desirability of a free flow of information and the recognition of the right of government and business to achieve their objectives in an efficient way.*[6]

In Australia, the law is developing faster – but also cautiously – to strengthen privacy and with one unusual legal decision. Just before the Google Spain judgment, the Australian Law Reform Commission suggested in an interim report a raft of amendments to privacy legislation, including a right to erasure. Under the 'Australian Privacy Principle', organisations over a specified size[7] would be required to take applications from individuals who wanted to remove information held about them, but would confine the process to deleting information which they had themselves supplied.

The report did not go as far as endorsing a regulatory agency having powers to compel a takedown of information in case of a dispute. Such a system 'may have an undesirably chilling effect on online freedom of expression' the commission said. The commission's final report dropped the proposal.[8]

In 2015, an Australian judge took the unusual step of classifying Google as a 'publisher', a move which if it turns out to be a lasting precedent will have important implications for the search engine. This is the status which Google has always avoided claiming, except occasionally in jurisdictions such as the US, where it has clear legal advantages. Like many defamation cases, the origins of this one lay in a bizarre and obscure dispute. Dr Janice Duffy had consulted psychics and commented on them in an online discussion forum. Other posts had been insultingly critical of her and these posts turned up high in Google searches on Dr Duffy's name. Google were asked to de-index the posts and refused.

Dr Duffy did not sue the authors or the forum: she sued Google. After a six-year legal fight, the judge found the search engine to be the responsible publisher and awarded Dr Duffy A$100,000 (£50,000) and costs. If the judgment is not successfully appealed, search engines visible in Australia face either taking their own editorial view about libel risks or, at the least, taking material down as soon as they are on notice that someone claims they have been defamed.

In October 2014, a Tokyo court ordered Google to remove more than a hundred search results which linked a man to crime. Tomohiro Kanda, the lawyer for the complainant, said that judges clearly had the EU judgment in mind. He has since been bombarded by requests from potential clients who want the same thing. A few months earlier Japan's largest search engine, Yahoo, had reviewed its policies after winning a court case against a claimant who had also wanted to take down links about a criminal past. Yahoo Japan later announced that it would process requests to delink in ways very similar to Google in Europe, weighing requests against criteria such as whether the person concerned is a public figure. 'The right to be forgotten has arrived in Japan,' said Hiroshi Miyashita, a professor at Chuo University in Tokyo.[9]

But the effects of the idea of a right to be forgotten vary in impact according to the history of a particular legal and political culture. Petitions for orders against malicious internet postings were multiplying before Google Spain: from 33 to the Tokyo District Court in 2009 to 711 in 2013. Privacy rights are not clearly established in Japanese law, but developed by cases. Politicians are litigious. Kenta Yamada, professor of media law and journalism at Senshu University, saw a dangerous precedent in the Tokyo court order:

> *Japan is unique in the world in that politicians are quick to sue the media for defamation. It does not matter if they win the cases or not. It is a form of threat, and can easily lead to self-censorship on the part of the media. The October injunction could fuel that trend.*[10]

South Korea has been energetically debating online privacy for years: large-scale data leakage scandals, communications interception by intelligence agencies, and controversial privacy invasions have all contributed to worries about risks lurking in online communications which had been enthusiastically welcomed by a population well-equipped with digital devices. In 2014, 20 million credit card accounts at three leading companies were hacked. But Korea has been for some time ranked as 'one of the toughest jurisdictions for data privacy compliance in the world'.[11] The Korean Communications Commission has appointed a task force to examine the issues prompted by the new push given to the 'right to be forgotten'. A spokesman for the commission told the *Financial Times* that they were under no obligation to follow the EU lead but 'the feeling is that Korea needs to follow the trend'. Any tightening or extension of the law will be argued over. Liberal politicians claim that politicians and business figures are already using the country's strict online defamation laws to sanitise their reputations and avoid scrutiny.

Latin America

What the Google Spain case did was to re-energise data protection law, even where the judgment did not directly apply. Mexico has had a data protection law since 2010 which recognises a 'cancellation right' for digital information, but until 2014, it was rarely successful. There were only 125 cancellation requests between 2012 and 2015 and only a quarter of those required arbitration by the regulator. But in 2015, an emboldened data protection authority started legal proceedings against Google for refusing a delisting request. The law allows sizeable fines in a case of non-compliance. Google said that the authority's ruling inhibited free speech; the authority claimed that no argument for public interest in retaining the information link had been made.[12]

A northern state governor had also petitioned a local paper to erase or delink a picture of his naked torso on its site. A Spanish company, Eliminalia, whose website claims 'we erase your past', has set up an office in Mexico. The site also says:

> When you hire our services, we track across the network any information, article or comment to appear on the same about you or your company and locate all the information, positive or negative. You can also give us the specific information you want to be removed, and we will delete such information from internet.[13]

The leader in the Spanish-speaking world – and perhaps the world as a whole – has been Argentina, whose legal challenges and initiatives began before those in Europe. Latin American codes of rights tend to emphasise ideas like personality and reputation alongside privacy more strongly than some European codes and they are markedly different from US-influenced ones. Most of the several hundred cases in the Argentine courts have been pursued by a single lawyer in Buenos Aires, Martin Leguizamon, and concern internet search links to pictures, often of celebrities. These are largely cases where the complainant wants a search engine to take down a link but they are usually using reputation, defamation, privacy, or copyright law rather than one which specifically provides for a right to be forgotten. A large number of celebrities succeeded in having pictures de-indexed, particularly where the images had appeared on porn sites without their permission. The footballer Diego Maradona was among those who managed to block some Yahoo links to his name from being visible in Argentina in 2008.

But as elsewhere, the higher courts have been reluctant to expand the right to be de-indexed when a test case has reached them. In 2009 a singer, dancer and actress Virginia Da Cunha sued both Google and Yahoo for linking her name and picture without her permission to websites with pornographic content. She alleged harm had been done to her rights of personality, reputation, and privacy.

The first judge to hear the case observed that both Google and Yahoo filtered their searches to automatically remove references to pornography; Yahoo had a filter specifically aimed identifying adult-only websites. Neither search engine indexed the whole web: links were blocked because of local laws, contracts, or at user request. The judge saw the key issue in the case being freedom of expression rights against the right of an individual to control the use of their image. The latter right was not explicitly protected in the Argentine constitution but is mentioned in four international rights codes.[14] The judge cited a law professor who argued that the right to control one's internet data includes a right to prevent others from using one's picture. The professor was arguing for other changes to Argentine law which taken together would have made a right to be forgotten.

The judge found for Da Cunha, and ordered modest fines against the search engines for 'moral damage' and that the porn links be taken down. An appeal court reversed this. All three judges were sympathetic to individuals injured by inaccurate information but two held that search engines could not be held liable for what appeared on sites to which they linked. The judge in the minority argued that search engines are not only passive carriers of information but active in selecting data for people to see. In this they are capable of doing harm and should be accountable for it.

In the 1990s, Argentina had joined other Latin American states in the *habeas data* movement which encouraged governments to adopt data privacy and protection laws as well as ones on freedom of information. The law protected misuse of one's picture as well as defending 'honour' and privacy. The constitution was amended to give rights to inspect personal data and legal grounds to request the 'suppression, rectification, confidentiality or updating' of personal data. It was not only in Europe that rights of data protection were broadly drawn. By the time laws in these areas had been strengthened by both amendment and court judgments, Argentina had one of the most complete sets of legal defences for privacy and data in the world.

But although the mentions of countervailing rights tend to be brief, the higher courts put them in the balance. In 2010, the television personality and model Maria Belen Rodriguez had won damages for linking her name to porn sites and, four years later, that case went to the Supreme Court. The judges made clear that the issue was one of broad rights in collision: freedom of speech and its 'incommensurable' value to democracy against rights to honour and personal image. The court ruled against Ms Belen Rodriguez, saying that the search engines were not liable if they did not have knowledge of the harmful material or if, once informed, they removed it promptly. The judgment was followed by two others of similar kind.

Routes towards legal protections online have varied. Some states have advanced a right to be forgotten; others have converged on the same point by strengthening privacy, copyright, reputation, and defamation laws. In Argentina in 2013 and 2014, four separate bills were introduced which would have widened powers to filter, de-index, or block internet content; none have so far made it to the statute book. In 2015, the Colombian supreme court followed several European precedents and confirmed that the identities of people convicted of crime were not to be published once a sentence had been served. Chile is in the process of passing a new data protection law based on the EU template. Several countries have put *habeas data* provisions on the Latin American model in their constitutions,[15] but they are expensive and time-consuming procedures to pursue; others have adopted data protections laws and set up regulators based on the European model.[16] Some have done both.

The battles over the internet and privacy in Brazil illustrate not only the volatile changes of political opinion but also how legislative arguments are mixed up with government attempts to mount surveillance with the help of search engines. In 2014, Brazil adopted an internet law which had been developed by intensive and open consultation and was widely praised, the Marco Civil Da Internet.[17] By the next year, politicians were aiming to amend it with a draft law called, less eloquently, PL215. The authors of PL215 are explicit that they are hoping to imitate the EU right to be forgotten and are hoping to change the balance of the law by gutting key provisions in the Marco Civil.

But attempts at imitation do not always deliver identical results. Freedom of expression would be 'shrunk', three internet NGOs wrote to the authors of the draft bill, complaining about the 'elasticity' of the words defining content which could be taken down.[18] As the campaigning Electronic Frontier Foundation put it:

> *While the CJEU [Court of Justice of the European Union] only concerned itself with delisting content from specific search engine search terms, PL215 gives the courts a blanket ability to require any site to take down content, using the vaguest of justification, and with no requirement to take into account current public interest, newsworthiness, critical review, or the need for an accurate historical record. There's no process for the decision to be challenged, no put-back process, no requirement that the deletion be minimized, nor any assurance that erroneous or malicious deletion requests be penalized. As dozens of Brazilian lawyers and activists have explained to the drafters, PL215 gives those with a vested interest in editing away critical commentary from news sites, blogs, archives and conversation – almost limitless power to re-edit the Net as they see fit.*[19]

Russia and the US

Nowhere are politicians keener to edit the internet than among the elite gathered around Vladimir Putin in Russia. When members of the Duma introduced a 'right to be forgotten' bill, they referred enthusiastically to Google Spain. The new Russian law which came into effect in January 2016 adopts some of the European Court's language and then goes further. The bill was passed with a large majority.

The new law says that search engines must stop linking to information which is 'inaccurate and dated, [or] which has lost meaning ... by virtue of any subsequent events'. But there is no mention of freedom of expression (let alone as a balancing factor in delisting decisions) and no exception for information about someone who is a public figure or for personal information which may be disclosed in the public interest. Search engine duties are left vague: the law does not make clear whether they are at risk of legal action in linking to any information about someone or just searches on her or his name.[20]

Russia's largest search engine Yandex complained that the law is unconstitutional (the Russian constitution includes a clause guaranteeing the right to seek and receive information), could take an 'eternity' to implement, and may not be technically feasible. Galina Arapova, of Russia's Centre for Media Rights, notes that the law may be incompatible with the European Convention on Human Rights and that its loose test on relevance will be attractive to politicians looking to sanitise what comes to the top of internet searches for their name:

> A year later, the situation will change, and it [a broken link] may become relevant again. A person who did not want to go into politics will suddenly decide to go there, and then all that was in his life will become more than relevant.[21]

The United States is the world's outlier. It has no general law of privacy or of data protection, although legal actions involving both are possible and specific laws deal with particular protections, such fairness in credit reporting or medical confidentiality. Defamation in the US is hard-going for plaintiffs taking on news organisations and others who claim the strong protection of the First Amendment. Most American legal experts specialising in First Amendment law think that a right to be forgotten, if attempted, would be taken to the Supreme Court and ruled unconstitutional.

Courts tend to give the benefit of the doubt to free speech. Actions claiming invasion of privacy usually failed if they were judged to be news. In an important precedent in 1993 a higher court ruled that a person does not have 'a legally protected right to a reputation based on the concealment of truth'.[22]

Attempts at what will readily be called censorship have to jump a high bar. Quite right, said the internet scholar Jonathan Zittrain, who says there are certainly privacy problems online but the only safeguard against a correction system going wrong is open criteria for de-indexing and a reviewable process – which EU law does not provide. Zittrain predicts that negotiations about de-indexing will eventually be conducted on both sides by robots using artificial intelligence.[23]

7

New Law: The General Data Protection Regulation

In 2010, the European Commission launched a lengthy consultation on revising data protection law. In the 15 years since the original directive had been agreed a lot had changed. That text had been written in a world of mainframe computers which, in recent memory, had worked with punched cards. When the first data protection directive was adopted in 1995, Google had not been incorporated as a company. The new law which the Commission was generating in 2010 would work in a world of supercookies and social networks.

In 2012, the Commission revealed its principal ideas, including the proposal that what had been a directive ought to become a regulation, a stricter form of EU law which leaves national governments less room for discretion or manoeuvre in their own jurisdictions. The announcement included a suggestion that the EU should legislate for a right to be forgotten.

The General Data Protection Regulation (GDPR) was finalised in 2016 and will enter force in 2018, most probably without ever coming into force in the UK. The regulation covers many purposes in an attempt to boost, modernise and harmonise the powers of individuals to control the collection and processing of information about them. At least one legislature has anticipated it. In January 2016, the French national assembly adopted a 'Digital Republic' bill. The law anticipates the GDPR, including a stronger provision for individuals to ask for online material to be de-indexed or erased. The new version requires the search engine or other intermediary to de-index or take the material down immediately, before weighing any decision about whether the complaint is justified. If a month goes by without action, court action and fines can follow. The fines allowed are much larger than before, allowing the French data protection authority (CNIL) to:

> *pronounce fines up to EUR 20,000,000 or 4% of a company's global turnover (whichever is higher) if a data controller fails to comply with the*

> Data Protection Act. This is a significant enhancement from the maximum €150,000 fine the CNIL may pronounce under the current law.[1]

The French law draws on the GDPR. The outline of that law proposed by the Commission in Brussels in 2012 drew heavily on the earlier version of data protection. Whatever the new references to social networks and sharing, it is still shaped by the ideas born in the era in which a company held information about a person in filing cabinets. Some laws stand the test of time, but the ideas behind data protection have not done so, leaving the law both lopsided in principle and ill-equipped for the new challenges presented by technology.

The issues of large-scale, frictionless sharing of personal memories, quarrels, celebrations, and news is treated at the margins. Despite nods towards other rights, the GDPR text makes clear that the protection of personal privacy outranks freedom of expression or knowledge. Aware that data are more fluid and mobile than ever before, the emphasis of the text and its accompanying explanations has shifted from protecting a person 'owning' her or his personal data to stressing an individual's ability to 'control' it wherever it may be.

Article 17

Different intentions cluster behind the multifaceted idea of a right to be forgotten. Over time, and most particularly after Google Spain, the text on deleting or obscuring internet content was toughened. The text reflects majority, but by no means universal, understanding of where the boundaries between data protection, privacy, and free expression lie. Experience with earlier data protection law has shown that opinion across 28 political cultures on this kind of issue does not tend to converge. Opinion on the diagnosis of the problem is clear – personal data is increasingly often at risk – but agreement on prescriptive remedies is elusive.

The key provision, Article 17, is called the 'right to erasure' ('right to be forgotten'). It opens with a broad right which is then gradually defined and qualified:

> The data subject shall have the right to obtain from the controller the erasure of personal data concerning him or her without undue delay and the controller shall have the obligation to erase data without undue delay where one of the following grounds applies:

The grounds are: where the data is 'no longer necessary' to the original purpose of collection, the data subject withdraws consent, he or she objects to the processing or the data has been illegally processed. The 'controller' – such as a search engine, Facebook or Twitter – is also obliged to take 'reasonable steps' to inform other data controllers who may have the information that someone has asked to take it down. Contrary to many legal systems elsewhere in the world, the erasure or de-indexing is done straight away. Daphne Keller of Stanford University[2] (and previously a Google lawyer) sees this as an invitation to misuse:

> As a matter of fair process even in run-of-the-mill cases, this automatic restriction right is troubling. An allegation made in secret to a private company should not have such drastic consequences. In other, less common – but all too real – scenarios, it is flatly dangerous. Instant, temporary removal of internet content is a tool begging for use by bad actors with short-term issues: the disreputable politician on the eve of election; the embezzler meeting a new client; the convicted abuser looking for a date. Mandating it by law is a big mistake.[3]

These rules do not apply if the processing is for 'exercising the right of freedom of expression and information', required under the law or public health policy or for 'archiving in the public interest' or scientific, historical, or statistical purposes. Until the GDPR comes into force and is tested in decisions in national courts, the effect of this new wording is hard to predict. But the tests for removing links remain loosely drawn and relatively easy to pass. The exceptions, such as for freedom of expression, have not proved particularly strong in the past.

The GPDR's references to freedom of speech and the public interest are an improvement on previous versions. They are further strengthened by Article 80 which adopts language from the earlier law and hands to national governments of the EU the business of reconciling the rights involved:

> Member states shall by law reconcile the right to the protection of personal data pursuant to this Regulation with the right to freedom of expression and information, including the processing of personal data for journalistic purposes and the purposes of academic, artistic or literary expression.

The caveats, if faithfully reproduced in national laws and weighed both by data authorities and courts, may be enough to restore some balance of rights. There will be further interpretations, particularly from the data authorities in the Article 29 Working Party, but court cases will settle the question. The strengthened and welcome references to both freedom of expression and the public interest in the text probably reflect three influences.

First, the public and political reaction to Google Spain underlined how sensitive the issue of 'censoring' the news media by taking down Google links could be, at least in parts of the EU. Second, judges in a handful of countries[4] handed down judgments on fights between complainants, search engines, and data protection authorities which implied that they thought the 'right' given by Google Spain was too generous. Third, the volume of de-indexing requests since the judgment combined with the rejection rate – running at roughly 60 per cent of the total – suggests that ill-founded requests are not at all unusual. Most cases which have reached national courts since Google Spain have shown judges to be fully conscious of the delicate rights questions which are at stake.

But there are difficulties for freedom of expression and information in the small print of the GDPR. That law had encouraged states to set up protection for freedom of expression in their own laws, but a comparative study in 2013 showed an inconsistent mixture of measures, some of them weak.[5] Three EU states have no freedom of expression provisions at all in their data protection law.[6]

In the context of tension between free speech and data protection, simple brief assertions of rights may not be enough. There are brief references to data processing protected from legal challenge because it is 'in the public interest'. This is a useful incentive to legislators (and a hint to judges interpreting law) but still a blunt instrument. Because the regulation will cover EU states and aims to harmonise law between all of them, no clearer definition of what the 'public interest' might mean proved possible, although it would have been desirable. Arguments in favour of a public interest exception or defence resonate in Britain and Scandinavia, but have little or no purchase in other parts of the EU. French lawyers and lawmakers are scornful and suspicious of a phrase which, in the view of many, functions only as a 'get out of jail free' card for unscrupulous journalists. Digital communications will multiply the challenges which societies – whatever their varied inheritance of culture and ideas – face along the disputed frontier between public and private. We will need to look again at whether the idea of public interest or public value help us resolve disputes at the border.

Takedown clauses

The takedown clauses outlined above are much tougher in a number of ways which make the erasing or de-indexing of legal content more likely. Internet intermediaries, likely to be the most frequent targets of requests, have only begun to deal with erasure or obscurity applications since Google Spain. Until then, procedures for handling them fell usually under the national laws developed from the 'e-commerce' directive or, in the US, from the Digital Millennium Copyright Act. These laws generally have more balanced procedures and the decisions are less delicate.

An individual who wants to scrub material which they have provided should have little problem in doing so and most large intermediaries such as Facebook do this.[7] Existing data protection law tends to assume that there is an actual (or implied) bilateral contractual relationship between the intermediary or platform and the person who feels harmed by content. The complications begin when the individual asks for the deletion of content about them by a third party. The law ought to balance the rights of four parties: the individual who is the subject of the material, the person who 'published' it, the intermediary who provides the platform or the link for it, and the public who may have an interest in knowing what it reveals.

Take the following example, which assumes that the GDPR is in force in the EU. A businessman who runs a prominent local firm in a rural area is addressing a dinner a few weeks before local elections. He makes an unpleasant joke about immigrants being likely to commit crime. The joke is offensive and unjustified, but not illegal. Someone at the dinner makes a smartphone video of parts of the speech. A short fragment of video appears on Twitter, but attracts little attention. One of the people who retweets it has Twitter set up so that the tweets appear automatically in her Facebook page.

Someone seeing that page realises that the businessman is the man who has discreetly funded the country's 'Leave the EU' campaign and writes an angry Facebook post on his own page linking to the video. The businessman applies to Google, Bing, and Yahoo to have them delink the video. He is not a public figure, he argues, and the dinner at which he spoke was not a public occasion. He reminds the search engines that they are obliged under the (new) law to take the link down while examining the case.

Any search engine, data protection authority or court ought to be weighing the interests of all four parties listed above. It is very doubtful that the GDPR has been written or structured so as to make that the likely outcome. Is the businessman a public figure? Is his personal data being 'processed', and if so, by how many parties? Who is the publisher and who the intermediary? Whose view should be heard on whether this ought to remain retrievable in the public interest? Who are, in the words of EU data protection law, the 'data controllers' here? Is the law right to bite on the processing of data rather than on its collection?

Intermediaries

Google Spain has brought search engines, and most probably other intermediary platforms, firmly under data protection law as data controllers. Defenders of Google Spain and the right to be forgotten argue that search engines are held responsible for their own activities in linking, and in particular for the profile of a person assembled by their links. No threat is posed to the original content, to its author or publisher, or to freedom of speech. The separation of the search engine from the original material is central to the court judgment. This is a distinction without a difference. If information can only be found via a search engine, the intermediaries both have responsibilities and a significant role in freedom of expression and the right to know.

As Professor Jack Balkin writes, 'the hallmark of the digital age is a revolution in the infrastructure of free expression'.[8] The ways in which free speech travels requires some re-engineering of how that speech is protected. Much of the concern about this has been about state surveillance and protection from it. But Balkin's point applies equally to situations where state surveillance is not an issue but where the intermediary is under pressure effectively to regulate or over-regulate ordinary speech. Balkin calls this 'collateral censorship':

> Collateral censorship occurs when the state holds one private party A liable for the speech of another private party B, and A has the power to block, censor, or otherwise control access to B's speech. This will lead A to block B's speech or withdraw infrastructural support from B. In fact, because A's own speech is not involved, A has incentives to err on the side of caution and restrict even fully protected speech in order to avoid any chance of liability.

That example uses state censorship as illustration. But the same issue arises between the state, the individual and a private-sector intermediary. From the time that Google Spain began to be implemented by the search engines themselves, one worry has been that private-sector intermediaries might always take the cautious choice and remove content when in doubt. It remains unclear whether under the GDPR any interested party, such as a publisher or a member of the public, could take court action to restore a de-indexed link. There may be no effective check on those who err on the side of caution. The risk of caution is greater when the search engine has fewer resources to sift hard decisions.

The process which data protection law enforces requires an intermediary such as Google to, if necessary, defend a decision to retain a link when they may know less about why it was published than the original author or publisher. But if an intermediary refuses to delink and is challenged, the next stage of the dispute is between the data protection authority (DPA) and the intermediary and it is confidential. Publisher and author have no role or access. The linkage is the immediate issue but that is so fundamental for access to the information that it is unfair and unreasonable to deny the publisher or author the right to intervene.

Some data protection authorities are well-equipped to protect free speech; others less so. Daphne Keller sees this as a basic flaw of the GDPR:

> *The GDPR's provisions for DPA and court enforcement replicate many of the problems of the notice and takedown process: responsibility for defending or assessing free expression rights rests with entities that lack the information or incentives to reach a fair outcome, while people who do have information and incentives to defend their expression are excluded from the process.*[9]

In contrast to the anxieties expressed by news publishers and free speech advocates, archivists and historians who have looked at the new law hope that they are protected by exemptions. The British Library rests on a test written into the UK's Data Protection Act which says that individuals who want information taken down or de-indexed need to show evidence that they are suffering 'damage or distress'. Neither the directive now in force in the EU nor the draft GDPR actually make this requirement and the Google Spain judgment says that evidence of damage or distress is not required for de-indexing from a search engine.[10] A post from the British Library's head of web archiving pointed out that Google Spain applies only to search engine links and that the Library's regular 'snapshot' of the World Wide Web is not available for search engines.[11] The International Federation of Library Associations (IFLA) was warier, acknowledging the protections for archives but also stressing that it was waiting to see how new law was applied in practice.[12]

The British Library, like many other organisations on the web, carries a standard notice on its site of 'notice and takedown' procedures. Until Google Spain and the writing of the GDPR, these notice and takedown guidelines were the most frequently found procedures for complaint to a website. The EU itself built them into a different directive (on e-commerce) which attempted to ensure that internet platforms were not held automatically liable for content which they carried. Broadly, they would be protected from legal action if, when warned that content was illegal, offensive, or harmful, they took prompt action. Which directive determines EU law on takedown or de-indexing is not yet clear.

Fearing that the protection of intermediaries was being undercut by new law (including the GDPR) and court judgments, a multinational group of free speech and internet rights organisations wrote the 'Manila Principles'[13] as an attempt to balance the rights of individuals harmed by online information, authors, publishers, and the intermediaries who carry or link to it.

Two of those organisations criticised the GDPR for its

> *harsh yet vague procedure that it institutes for the automatic and immediate restriction of content about an individual by an intermediary, when it receives a request for the restriction of that content by that individual – even if it the content was provided by a third party. This conflicts with the Manila Principles, which provide that laws should not require the intermediary to take action on a content restriction order or request until so ordered by an independent and impartial judicial authority.*[14]

On this view the takedown procedures written into the GDPR are about to become some of the toughest of their kind in the world. How far the regulation will hold intermediaries responsible remains murky. The text says that intermediaries are still protected from being held liable for third-party content under the provisions of a different directive (also scheduled for revision). The most onerous duties in the GDPR apply to 'data controllers' who make active decisions and are not passive conduits. But this distinction is being blurred as intermediaries take value from data as it passes through their hands.

On the relevance and significance of a piece of personal information across time, the GDPR makes almost no change. It expresses the apparently reasonable idea of 'purpose limitation' – that data should not be retained when the reason for its collection has expired – but leaves it to data protection authorities and the courts to make detailed decisions. This long-established principle, reproduced in data protection all over the world, suffers from a basic weakness: it cannot deal with the fact that a single piece of information is of different value to different people at different times of the information's life. The compromise built into Google Spain – that it took the information out of internet search but did not delete the newspaper archive – was in part aimed at delivering obscurity short of deletion.

But what the judgment did not cover was what would happen if circumstances in the future made the information about Sr Costeja more relevant.[15] Supposing that in 2020 Sr Costeja decided to run for public office in Barcelona. Re-indexing a piece of information is presumably no harder than de-indexing. Even if relisting can happen, reversing a de-indexation requires knowing what information has been obscured. Sometimes that is available, sometimes it is hard to piece together. The significance of the information about Sr Costeja's previous debts might be considered once again significant, having in 2014 been reckoned old enough to de-index.

Geography matters. That brush with bankruptcy might be relevant to people in Barcelona who are choosing among candidates, but it would hardly be important to people in Helsinki or Hanoi who, thanks to a World Wide Web, are equally able to retrieve it. But if Sr Costeja was to pursue a new career in Spanish politics and if he became Prime Minister, exercising responsibilities not only in Madrid but in the whole EU, then people in Helsinki might well be interested in his background. The public value of information alters both in time and in space.

How law and societies are to deal with 'black box' algorithmic issues such as the right to be forgotten pose a test of agility for governments and particularly for the unwieldy policy-making of the EU. Digital technology will not stop changing and will generate new dilemmas. 'Future-proofing' policy and law becomes harder as technology change accelerates. As one critic sums up:

> *The data protection system evolved to provide transparency and accountability on government and industrial databases. It has simply not adapted appropriately to the realities of the information age. Perversely the indiscriminate operation of data protection rules serves as a disincentive to start-ups and small businesses and, at the same time, a triviality to incumbents.*[16]

Wired societies have not yet grappled with whether we can find ways which fit our ideas about fairness, memory, and forgiveness to adjust information for permanence or accessibility. 'The last three years of debate about the GDPR should have been about the future and not about the small print,' the UK's Information Commissioner Christopher Graham said in 2015.[17] We have so far assumed, because those have been the technical solutions so far offered, that information may be permanent and can and should all be found or that it should be deleted. Google Spain added a third option: a variable degree of obscurity. The speed with which technology develops may offer fresh choices.

8

Alternative Approaches

Disagreements about the right to be forgotten are ones of prescription, not of diagnosis. Widespread agreement exists that the internet has brought with its many advantages a problem of harm caused by its efficiency in accumulation and retention. In the vast sediment of information which we now have, a small proportion can do damage. Unfair and inaccurate information has always passed between people, but in the twenty-first century the ability to preserve it and find it has outstripped the rate at which it might once have been forgotten or lost. The debate about the right to be forgotten captures the issue of what principles we should use to decide what information we do not wish to keep or make easy to find and who should decide that. It is the argument of this study that the European data protection framework is a poorly designed and unbalanced instrument for resolving this question. Are there other, better ways?

One piece of the answer must be algorithms. The strings of code which search the web may operate automatically, but they are created by humans who choose and adjust which indicators of prominence will get what weight in the instant calculation. Even if the algorithms teach themselves to improve how they do this (by using feedback from internet users for example), human intervention is still part of the process.

When Sr Costeja searched Google years after his financial difficulties, he felt that the algorithm was unfair by dredging up something so old. In his view, the retrieval was inefficient and had failed. The law allowed him to punish the failure because Google would not delete the link. Google, although it was not asked to do this, would surely have been equally unwilling to set the precedent of adjusting, on request, the prominence of a search result.

Whether the right to be forgotten is a good or bad idea, Google Spain has helped us to see beyond the early, miraculous nature of internet search. If I enter 'right to be forgotten' in Google, I get 2,050,000 results in 0.74 seconds.[1] I have no idea how Google has ranked those results and like most people I rarely delve past the first page of results. I have no exact idea how Google's formulae have ranked those links, partly because the algorithms are Google's trade secret and partly because they evolve. I have some hazy clues: weight will be given to how many people link to a site, some attention will be paid to what I have searched before and the engine will know where I am. If I want to know more, I can always search for background on search techniques and developments and it will produce enough to keep me busy reading for weeks.

Friction

Sizeable amounts of research are conducted in universities, private companies, and governments on refining search.[2] If we want to avoid deleting information because of its possible future usefulness, we may wish to make, in carefully defined conditions under the law, requirements as to how easy or hard certain items of information will be to find. As information scientists put it, we would increase the 'friction' involved in finding information that was liable to be harmful or distressing with low or no public value. American lawyers invented the term 'practical obscurity' to cover information which would not disappear but which would be harder to find. Google Spain has now made the auction of Sr Costeja's house and furniture not invisible but almost impossible to find. Is it likely that search engines can adjust for relative degrees of obscurity if required?

It seems at least possible that a one-size-fits-all information retrieval system might become more subtle over time. Even if this does become technically possible, that would not settle the question of the criteria which would amend algorithms to demote or promote particular pieces of information or whether individuals would have power to compel such changes and under which conditions. Would a search engine be more useful to its users if it pushed down items more than 10 years old? Not to historians. Reputation management companies promise that kind of editing, but their services are only available to those able to afford them.

Reducing the salience of a search result is a form of 'friction' which makes information harder to find without hiding it. The internet has changed the relationship between the existence of information and its accessibility. Books in a library are both available and accessible in the same place at the same time. Online information exists, but its existence has become decoupled from availability or access. To make any use of the existence of information, the user must have the means to find the needle in the haystack. Once that assistance was a card index; now it is algorithms and servers owned and operated on the other side of the globe by a multi-national corporation. So far, search engines have concentrated on solving the problem of sorting information in a split second. Is it possible to imagine that, as the world's stock of data grows, some of it may be ranked by criteria which include public stipulations about fairness, accuracy or relevance?

What other kinds of information 'friction' might be possible? Might archives which are comprehensive make some information simply and easily available while erecting barriers around some knowledge which might be controversial or contested – or simply flagged as such? This would be a decision to raise the cost of reaching the information, as an alternative to losing it completely. It might be a financial cost or a requirement to justify a request to see something. A database or archive which is instantly available to everyone is an attractive ideal, but as data increase and the complications of permanence increase, that aim may not continue to be the ideal.

One reputation management company, Digitalis, already claims to have software which will detect for a client changes in the conditions which affect search engine rankings for a link, so they can spot, and try to reverse, any unwanted rise in an unwelcome link. A reputation management company does this as a private, commercial transaction. Could a regulator require such changes as a matter of policy? But any such measure would have to take some account of both the rights and different needs of different searchers. People search as employers, employees, voters, customers, lovers, cyber-trolls, the idly curious, and in many other roles besides.

Fragments

One aspect of search is almost bound to change over time and it should have the effect of making search results a better picture of the world. Many complaints about algorithmic search concern the disconnected and fragmentary nature of what is returned. Old information is not linked to newer data or more up-to-date versions. As we have seen, many requests to have information corrected or delinked which concern journalism turn on the issue of whether the full sequence of events in criminal investigations or trials has been reported. News media in many jurisdictions have long accepted restrictions which require the reporting of trials to be balanced between both sides.³ Does the permanence of digital information suggest that news media should accept a similar responsibility to complete a story which begins with a police inquiry or charge?

Information is often stripped of context which supplies perspective and meaning. Irrespective of the arguments generated by a right to be forgotten, computer science has enormous incentives to enhance search to make it more efficient and effective. Most search engines currently return far more information than the searcher needs. One of the strongest demands is for search which filters out less relevant or significant information – judgements which are hard, but not impossible, to express in algorithms. Enriching context or making it more coherent will not solve the problem of information which someone wants deleted or who thinks that linking it at all is unfair, but it will reduce the chance of random fragments distorting the truth.

Other software-based solutions have been canvassed. Could personal and private information be protected by a version of the techniques used to protect material under copyright, known as digital rights management (DRM)? This solution suffers from a number of drawbacks. Intellectual property to be protected needs to be tagged with meta-information which identifies it. It requires a legal infrastructure to catch evasion and to back up the owner's rights. All such information is not protected at the moment of consumption – the showing of a film, for example – when it can be copied.⁴

Others have suggested various kinds of building in an automatic time expiry option for text and pictures. Start-ups like Snapchat, Tigertext, Secret, or Whisper all use perishable material as their selling point: text and picture simply delete themselves after a set time. A system with more discretion would allow anyone creating a document or post to be offered the chance to allow it to disappear after a specified time. Viktor Mayer-Schönberger, endorsing this idea as a way of 'reintroducing forgetting', hopes that a competitive momentum could be set up by the powerful players. He cites the bidding war which followed Google's announcement in 2007 that it would anonymise the search queries it holds after two years. After other search engines had followed suit but with shorter intervals, Google shortened the interval to nine months. But the technical challenges of building expiry into every kind of information which an individual can put online are considerable. No one knows how much use such an option would get.

A project from the University of Washington called Vanish illustrates the technical difficulties of turning that kind of simple idea into a robust, user-friendly tool for everyday use. The 'Vanish' project, still under way, aims to give anyone sending information across the web a way of ensuring that the data, wherever they are stored or copied, self-destruct after a set time. In the words of the project's designers:

> Specifically, we wish to ensure that all copies of certain data become unreadable after a user-specified time, without any specific action on the part of a user, without needing to trust any single third party to perform the deletion, and even if an attacker obtains both a cached copy of that data and the user's cryptographic keys and passwords.[5]

The first version of this software was hacked by engineers from three other universities in a counter-project called 'Unvanish'.

The world wide web's founder, Tim Berners-Lee, is working on a project called Solid ('social linked data') which would allow internet users to store information in 'pods' and they would be able to control access to that data by applications or social networks.[6] The network Diaspora was originally designed and spread as a user-owned network and social platform decentralised enough, via many dispersed servers, to protect the privacy of its users. The implied contrast was with Facebook. But when the online members of Islamic State (IS) were forced off Facebook and Twitter, they began posting on Diaspora, whose network was decentralised to the degree that no one could take down IS posts.[7]

Whether governments intervene to promote competition or whether it happens naturally, competition in search over time is likely to increase. Greater competition ought to increase the rate of innovation and speed up the search for easier ways to adjust results to avoid harm. Taking a different tack, American commentators and legislators have given thought to ways in which someone can 'reset' their digital life – assuming that they can be confident that they can delete the version they want to lose. These are mostly in the uncontroversial area of content posted by an individual who wants to take it down and not in the harder area of third-party material. California has passed a law allowing those under 18 to have a legal right to void their social network postings, in an attempt to lower the risk that mistakes made while young will not follow people into adulthood.[8] Jonathan Zittrain proposed that the young and old might want a right to declare 'reputational bankruptcy', to be able to cancel their online career and start all over again.[9]

Few of the proposals in this chapter are likely to work unless underpinned by law. High-tech companies provide benefits, but resist regulation as robustly as any others. It is tempting to think that technology will provide solutions to social dilemmas, but usually wrong. Technology may help, but society has to reach a decision about the balance between privacy and disclosure which sets the framework in which technology can work.

Online news

The Google Spain judgment was not directly aimed at the news media, although the controversial minority of the delistings have often been news stories whose links have gone. The approaches of news media to requests for archived stories to be moved out of view will probably evolve over time. We will learn relatively little of this as it happens, for a reason which online news media are reluctant to discuss more often than they have to.

Online news sites are magnets for the malicious. When broadcast and print media first went online in the 1990s, prevailing wisdom among online gurus and editors held that interactivity with readers would be a crucial area of development in journalism and that a vehicle for this would be comments at the foot of news and comment articles. The crowd is wiser than the individual writer, this school of thought predicted, and journalism will be better for the wisdom of the crowd. Interactivity and a wider participation has had many good effects. But, with rare exceptions, not in comments beneath news and opinion articles. By 2015, a number of major news sites were closing their articles to comments altogether.[10] Users were getting little value from comments, as they made clear. Administering comment strands was becoming more and more burdensome and occasionally legally dangerous. In the worst cases, writers and contributors were harassed and insulted.

Gradually, news sites are becoming a little less 'open'. Registration is more common to be able to comment, often via a social network which makes being anonymous or taking a false identity harder. Sites have got more sophisticated about spotting attempts to ruin or hijack discussion forums. Legal risk management has improved. Algorithms which trigger alerts when a comment is liable to breach site rules work better. Editors, by watching the spread of concern about valueless or malign information, have become more sympathetic to requests to amend or even take down material they can't defend.

But editors will rarely talk or write about the subject in public. They are discreet about takedown procedures which they control for several reasons. They may experiment with guidelines and change them as they go along; they would prefer to avoid the charge of inconsistency. If Google delink a URL and a news site wants to protest, some disclose the fact.[11] But other editorial judgements about web content are dealt with more discreetly, not least from fear of triggering an avalanche of complaints which would be hard to handle.

The newsrooms of the *Guardian*, *El Pais*, and the online division of France Télévisions have all adjusted their procedures, gradually and discreetly, to deal more flexibly not only with the formal procedures for a right to be forgotten arising from Google Spain but to be broadly more sympathetic to people who claim to suffer from what they consider to be a hostile algorithm. The new rules at *El Pais* commit the paper to updating information as far as is possible on convictions when they are appealed or reversed. But they do not commit to taking news reports down – simply to updating. Delisting of links is possible for something which is more than 15 years old. Serious crime is not delisted. But any reader of their websites would have difficulty in finding evidence of that change.

Such adjustments to editorial policies are part of a wider trend. Journalists accustomed to the use of dusty newspaper or broadcast archives have gradually been made aware that indefinite retention and powers of retrieval alter the picture of the world that their users can see. News media sites tend to function on two levels. On the more familiar level, news and commentary are added every hour or every day. On the second level, a news site is a huge repository of fragments of news; those fragments are as immediately available to the user as the news of the moment. Google has conceded that a few of those fragments can cause unintended but clear harm, even if the precise number may be a matter of dispute. Some editors, whatever their reservations about Google Spain, have started to move in the same direction.

9

Conclusions: The Future

The pressure behind the right to be forgotten is partly a wish to turn the clock back to the pre-digital age. Google Spain ought to be the start, and not the end, of a debate over how to deal with new and unavoidable questions in new ways. Information has altered radically over two decades, by historical standards a very small interval for such a large transformation. One prominent global survey finds search engines a more trusted source of general news and information than the established news media.[1] There are many channels and routes by which we learn about things we cannot see and hear – there is more information, more sources generate knowledge, and it can be more easily shared and exchanged. The production of information has been dispersed and it is distributed both on one-to-many routes and many-to-many networks.

Power over information has thus changed shape and location. The cost of speaking in the public sphere has never been lower. But new quasi-monopolies act as gatekeepers and platforms in a reconstructed chain of information creation and consumption. The scale and velocity of information use has magnified the risk to individuals that information can be distributed and found which will do them harm which cannot be justified.

This study is about societies which value free expression and it asks if the 'right to be forgotten' poses any risk to that freedom in general and to journalism in particular. In one sense, the right to be forgotten is a subsection of the wider field of data protection, which is itself part of a larger set of what lawyers now call 'information rights'. But the right to be forgotten is important in itself and emblematic: the debate captures many important dilemmas which arise from the new ways in which we look for information and find it. If used carefully and proportionately, it ought not interfere with journalism's task of discovering, verifying, distributing, and storing information and opinion of public value. But the issue turns on care and proportion; the risk to journalism is clear.

Defences and justifications for free expression were divided by one authority into four groups: assisting self-fulfilment, the discovery or iteration of truth, assisting the working of democracy, and testing suspicions of government.[2] The exercise of the right of free expression has always been connected to the infrastructure of communication which makes real the right to distribute and seek information.[3] The question of how to make policy for the infrastructure of free expression is not only complex but volatile: that infrastructure keeps changing shape.

The high-tech giants of today provide things which millions people want and think they cannot do without. Those companies are now part of the infrastructure of free expression. When public communication was in print, governments once sought to control whatever was printed anywhere at any time. Gradually, the communication of knowledge – not least journalism – freed itself from state control. Digital communication democratised communication by offering easy means for anyone with a computer linked to the phone network to become a publisher. That same technology also created giant new information companies which are among the most valuable in the world. Both the state and society have been interested in controlling what they do. As Jack Balkin puts it:

> *Increasingly, speech regulation and surveillance are technologically imposed and involve cooperation between governments and private entities that control the infrastructure of free expression. Thus a feature of the early twenty-first century is that the infrastructure of free expression increasingly is merging with the infrastructure of speech regulation ...*[4]

Companies like Google continue to insist that they stand to one side of debates about free expression rights. From its foundation, the search engine stressed that it created no content, that it wanted to be useful by allowing people to reach the information they needed and, on the internet, could not find without help. No one should confuse Google, its spokesmen underline, with the 'media'.

To a point, this is plainly true. Google does not report: it does not create content like a news website, an opinion magazine, or a television channel. Google and Facebook regularly reiterate that what happens in their realms is controlled by their users; what they provide is the platform, the servers, and the computational power. But this is information power of another sort. One of the reasons that battles like the one over the right to be forgotten have erupted is that no one has quite decided what kind of power the high-tech companies have in the new infrastructure and how to manage it when the company's interest may conflict with the law or with the public interest.

A search engine is an intermediary between material and user. Accurate or undisputed statistics about the share of search for each company are not easily available, but by most estimates Google has a share of search in the US between 70 and 80 per cent; in Europe, its share in each country is mostly over 90 per cent.

That is near-monopoly power, achieved by Google's technical dominance, the efficiency of its searches. After Google Spain and in Europe, Google has a power, which it did not seek, to make the first call on a request for de-indexing. The company has lobbying power and it has market power over advertisers, who cannot operate outside of Google's advertising system. Above all, it has steadily been accumulating data power.[5] The official slogan may be 'don't be evil', but Google's reach and resources have seen it accused of sins ranging from privacy violation to provoking class warfare. Sr Costeja certainly believed that the pursuit of the aim to 'organise the world's information' was capable of causing harm.

Google and the law

Google's founders often sound bored and irritated by the ethical and legal disputes which their business generates. At a developers' conference in 2013, Google founder Larry Page gave a hint of his frustration with the world's unwillingness to realise how fast change is coming:

> *I think people naturally are concerned about change, and certainly not all change is good, and I think, I do think the pace of change in the world is changing. Part of what I would think about is, I would think that we haven't adapted mechanisms to deal with that. And maybe some of them are old institutions like the law and so on aren't keeping up with the rate of change that we've caused through technology.*

Law did not adapt fast enough:

> *If you look at the different kinds of laws we make, they're very old. The laws when we went public were 50 years old. A law can't be right if it's 50 years old, like it's before the Internet, that's a pretty major change.*[6]

Unfortunately, no member of Page's audience asked him if he thought that the First Amendment, adopted in 1791, had been rendered irrelevant by its antiquity. But his solution was that technologists should be able to try things out without legal consequences:

> *I think as technologists we should have some safe places where we can try out some new things and figure out what is the effect on society, what's the effect on people, without having to deploy kind of into the normal world. And people [who] like those kind of things can go there and experience that and we don't have mechanisms for that.*[7]

This wish to create a space safe from law, responsibility, or accountability hints at two beliefs which have been influential among developers of the internet: over-regulation risks stifling innovatory imagination and the closely related philosophy that the internet is a new freedom which cannot be under central control and should not be under any control at all. The first of these arguments deserves respect. The second would see the application of copyright laws to search engines as just as bad as law on the right to be forgotten and applied at vaster greater scale. But a great deal of evidence has accumulated in the past two decades that the internet is not a democratic instrument or institution but, like others before, a means of communication which can be used for good and bad. As such, we have to work out ways to maximise the former and minimise the latter. We will otherwise end up with a cyberspace whose true workings are opaque, inconsistently regulated (if at all), and determined by algorithms designed and controlled by a small number of private companies.

Lawmakers everywhere struggle to understand, keep up, and adapt. Search engines do not exercise editorial responsibilities, conventionally defined. They use others' content and point people to it. But their algorithms give access to information not otherwise available (except with disproportionate effort) and they rank it for display. They police content, according to various rules, depending on jurisdictions. They exercise discretion by creating and adjusting algorithms. One evening I see a television advertisement for Specsavers with the line 'search expert eyecare' on the last screen. Googling that phrase the next morning, I get a sponsored link for Specsavers at the top. Below that, the top three results are also for Specsavers; the four together fill the laptop screen.[8] Is this a coincidence? It may be, but many regulators on either side of the Atlantic think that search results are being manipulated in connection with advertising. That is one of the charges against Google being investigated in Brussels. Staff at the US Federal Trade Commission thought that search and advertising were mixed when they found in 2012 that Google was promoting its own services, and demoting competitors. (But the trade commissioners closed the investigation the following year.)

A search engine's responsibility is not that of a news site, a newspaper, or television channel. But they do have, and exercise, responsibilities which form part of the infrastructure of free expression. Google began by denying any form of normal editorial responsibilities. Events and reality have gradually eroded that state of denial. Facebook, which exercises the same kinds of quasi-editorial power, is only just beginning to emerge from its state of denial.[9] Facebook will tell you in some detail about its 'community standards', but very little about how many complaints it receives (thought to be above 2 million a week) and almost nothing about how its rules interact with national legislations across the globe. The clues which emerge are fragmentary. A Facebook user registered in Turkey, or identified by geo-location as being there, does not see a Kurdish flag in their feed.

Google has accepted that it has a role in trying to help journalism during a phase of disruption of the traditional business model for news publishing. It processes copyright takedowns on an industrial scale. Google Spain has been the most prominent court judgment which implied that Google was being unduly modest and that it had more control over information than it pretended. But it has not been the only court reluctant to accept that search engines are neutral conduits with minimal legal accountability. Even Google acknowledges that Google has behaved better since Google Spain; legal action was required to achieve it.

In a 2014 case in New York which involved the Chinese search engine Baidu, the judge was asked to consider whether a search engine conducted operations which were protected by the First Amendment. He thought they were:

> *The central purpose of a search engine is to retrieve relevant information from the vast universe of data on the Internet and to organize it in a way that would be most useful to the searcher. In doing so, search engines inevitably make editorial judgements about what information (or kinds of information) to include in the results and how and where to display that information. ... In these respects, a search engine's editorial judgement is much like any other familiar editorial judgements, such as the newspaper*

> *editor's judgement of which wire-service stories to run and where to place them in the newspaper.*[10]

A few months later, a California judge ruled that Google's search activities were constitutionally protected under the First Amendment.[11]

Google's reluctance to take shelter under this legal doctrine in Europe may have significantly altered the course of the Google Spain case. The company did not argue that its operations deserved freedom of expression protection under data protection law. Whether the outcome would have been different if it had taken this step, we cannot know.

Search engines, unlike internet service providers (ISPs), do things which involve wider social responsibility. The position that they are only private companies providing only technical, neutral services is untenable. Google's expert panel, convened after the Google Spain case and holding public 'hearings' across the continent, propelled the company into a new kind of debate and limelight, at least in Europe. The court's interpretation of data protection law on de-indexing requests actually gave Google a new practical, public responsibility.

Could regulation for search engines strike the balance between enforcing some responsibility and not disrupting their role in providing infrastructure for free expression? Google holds information gatekeeper power which, measured by the simple scale of its use, exceeds the reach of more conventional media organisations. Now that the processing of de-indexing requests has settled down, the company ought to consider, and publicly debate, ways to give greater voluntary transparency to as much as possible of its 'editorial' procedure. There are constraints: algorithms are commercially confidential, Europe's data protection authorities want to restrict opening up the decision-making on the right to be forgotten to protect the privacy of people making the requests. Search engines and social networks could reply that to make the new infrastructure of free speech transparent might itself chill that freedom. Do the mainstream news media practise this kind of transparency? It is difficult to believe that in the context of the unprecedented scale and influence of the high-tech companies that transparency cannot go further.

A number of American commentators, however sympathetic to the idea of a 'forget me' button to deal with the web's worst aspects, have worried that turning the high-tech giants into highly regulated corporations will slow the rate of innovation and discourage the start-up culture which produced Google in the first place. Columbia media and law scholar Tim Wu points out that regulation has a tendency to produce a stable series of monopolies and that regulation exacts the worst penalties on the smallest firms, who may also be the most potentially inventive. 'Global free expression requires young companies,' he says, 'Free speech is linked to the spirit of entrepreneurialism. Attempts to defend individual privacy might end up strengthening corporate giants.'[12]

Journalism

Data is mostly not news. Most data protection does not concern itself with any dilemmas over disclosure in the public interest. There are laws protecting personal data for good reason: digital data is easily misused or abused. As the American scholar Frank Pasquale says: 'To declare such technologies of reputation beyond the bounds of regulation is to consign myriad innocent individuals to stigma, unfairly denied opportunities and worse.'[13] But the origins and operation of data protection have given and still give too little attention to the rights of those who seek and search for information. Data protection, developed to deal with the risk to personal information in physical storage, was never intended to come into collision with the public interest purpose of journalism. But that conflict has occurred. To say that the right to be forgotten targets only search engine links and not the original publication does not reconcile the competing rights. Hyperlinks, imperfect as they may be, are fundamental to knowledge today. An algorithmic element can be part of editorial added value.[14]

Open societies function best when the default is freely circulating information limited only where absolutely necessary. That we have new volumes of information and new dangers with it does not mean that we have to abandon the principle that we modify freedom of expression and rights to knowledge only with care and reluctance. Sr Costeja enforced his rights to delist links about his past that he thought were out of date. But in such cases, the rights of those seeking information have also to be taken into account. To simplify the Google Spain case as Sr Costeja's David-versus-Goliath fight against the search giant is to leave the rights of others to information out of account.

The presumption in favour of disclosure and publication should remain the foundation of the new infrastructure of free expression. If two people are tried for a serious criminal offence and one is convicted and the other acquitted, a report of the trial will cover both defendants. The report ought not be obscured on request from the acquitted person who is unavoidably linked to the guilty one. This is important for journalism but also for society's wider knowledge and memory. Not every fact worth publishing is a headline; historians draw pictures of the past with material that may once have seemed trivial. In the words of the US Supreme Court in 2010: 'Most of what we say to one another lacks "religious, political, scientific, educational, journalistic, historical, or artistic value" (let alone serious value), but it is still sheltered from government regulation.'[15] Journalists must guard against the misuse of a right to be forgotten. The right now named in EU law for the first time is an extension of privacy and data protection which is too broad and blunt for the news media to accept without careful monitoring, debate and redesign. Different societies fix the boundaries of public facts in different places. The attempt to align them across the EU has created a risk, despite well-intentioned safeguards, that reporting and recording in the public interest can be harmed.

The future

A news media organisation in Europe might one day choose to take a 'strategic' case designed to change the way that the law is operated and understood. That case might reach the Court of Justice of the European Union or the (slightly more sympathetic) European Court of Human Rights. But failing that, how might governments or data protection authorities ensure that the right balance is struck between free speech and privacy, given that existing and future data protection law fails to do that well enough? Here are twelve points on which the debate should focus:

1. It remains a mystery how the various stakeholders in the EU system spent six years revising a directive in an attempt to bring it up to date and yet finished with a text so badly adapted to twenty-first-century technology and its use. Once, when information was analogue and local, the laws of physics created automatic privacy and forgetting; those assumptions no longer hold. So the first priority must be to find a more effective way to express guarantees of privacy in the digital age. Erik Brynjolfsson and Andrew McAfee express this as the need for: 'explicitly designed institutions, incentives, laws, technologies or norms about which information flows are permitted or prevented and which are encouraged or discouraged'.[16]
2. The internet scholar Lawrence Lessig divided issues of content control into four categories: law, norms, market, and code. Some of the

solutions which rely on code were discussed in Chapter 8. At the moment, the legal framework relies on only two options – by no means available everywhere – if you feel that you have been harmed by something unduly permanent and retrievable online: deletion or de-indexing. Could search engines agree to demote – but not de-index – links to criminal convictions (below a certain level of seriousness) after a specified interval (five years, ten years)? Could search engines agree to seek the agreement of the original publisher to meta-tag information indicating a dissatisfied complainant? Or simply link to material which outlines the disagreement? As time goes on, the original aim of search engines to organise information to make it findable will surely evolve. One obvious evolution is to be able to indicate whether or not information can be relied on, or at least where it is disputed. Some algorithms which determine search prominence include that in their ranking criteria, but implicitly and not explicitly.
3. Social networks, still in their infancy, may discover that, if keeping data makes them unpopular, they may be forced by market pressure to build expiry dates into information. The short history of such networks has shown that they may grow very fast when fashionable but collapse very quickly when they no longer meet a need. Surveys suggest that up to half of employers look at social network profiles when handling a job application; one recent study found that half of those had found information which had caused them to reject a candidate.[17] Expiration dates will not eliminate indiscretions which people later regret or suffer. But over the long term expiry might give an added appeal to intermediaries or networks building in automatic deletion or opportunities for amendment which would offset the risk of accumulating less data.
4. Google Spain led to one good result. Google has been forced to confront and take part in arbitrating privacy and forgetting issues, even if the delisting process is imperfect. The company has the resources to take the process of exploring the implications much further. Exploring how societies strike a balance between rights in a new information age may be less exciting than trying to work out how to extend internet connectivity to human colonies on the moon, but this is now part of the civic responsibilities of search engines.
5. After Google Spain, many commentators criticised the court for leaving the first decision-making about de-indexing to a private company. Was this not the job of data protection authorities or courts alone? In a perfect world, data protection authorities might do this sifting: it is a

job for which they are qualified. But unless the rate of requests falls permanently to an improbably low level, very few EU authorities have the resources. The European Court guessed correctly. The search engines have the pivotal role and will have to keep it.

6. Whatever the process, the present one is unbalanced. Neither the author, publisher, nor potential user of what might be obscured has any purchase on the decision. It may well be that the majority of the judgements being made by Google would never in practice involve such complications. While there are protections for journalism in EU law, those protections should also afford stronger rights to contest delisting decisions. These protections are present if and when a delisting decision comes before a data protection authority or a court. But for that to occur, the author, publisher, or potential user has to know that the decision is being taken. At the moment, there is no enforceable way for that to happen. The obstacle here is most likely to be Europe's data protection authorities rather than the search engines. In their attempt to give individual complainants power against large companies, they have effectively prevented any producer of information from being able to intervene.

7. If search engines like Google, Bing, and Yahoo are making these delicate decisions about information rights, a higher degree of transparency is essential.[18] Complete transparency would defeat the object of a request for greater privacy, but Google's decision process has so far been conducted with no external inspection at all, although a handful of decisions have been challenged at data protection authorities and in the courts. It is possible that further court cases may shed a little light on individual decisions. But there is still no systematic way to check how exactly Google, Bing, and Yahoo apply in practice the general principles they have outlined. The visibility and external check on the use of this power is especially important in the light of the immediate takedown process written into the GDPR, which carries a risk that smaller search engines may opt for cautious and quick decisions. One of the benefits which greater transparency might bring is more evidence about the weakness of the right to be forgotten (in cases where no public interest is engaged) as a means of obscuring or concealing information. Its weakness lies in the indiscriminate nature of the rules which, in a few cases, may not protect privacy well enough.

8. Search engines should amend their autocomplete policies to avoid needless offence and grief. Software which suggests how a link might be

found is not a vehicle of free expression or free speech which deserves protection in law. It is a convenience which can do harm.[19] Algorithms can defame or slander and can be adjusted to avoid that risk.
9. Article 80 of the new data protection regulation[20] encourages national governments to pass laws to protect free speech when they are transposing the new measures into law. The UK government is unlikely to come under the General Data Protection Regulation (GDPR) but it seems likely retain data protection law which may now develop independent of EU precedent. EU governments are constrained by their obligation to make any new law compatible with the regulation, but they too have an opportunity for governments to follow the lead of courts which have tried to make sure that data protection's sweeping powers are seen in the context of basic rights. Could a bold government follow the Swedish example and simply make its data protection law subordinate to press freedom laws?
10. Perhaps the most basic change of all would be a recognition that data protection law is stuck in the wrong place. This has not been for want of good intentions, but the law has failed to develop at EU level with a proper balance of rights – and European precedent has been influential all over the world. The combination of reaction against the data and surveillance traditions of Nazis and Communists with Mediterranean traditions of 'honour' and reputation, which have been the main drivers of data protection law until now, are not the best basis for the complex and intricate dilemmas of information-rich digital societies. Neither is the division between 'data controller' and 'data subject', which imposes an artificial shape on fluid and intricate network relationships and which largely ignores the role of third parties in handling information is out of date. While the imbalance of rights may have been, and may still be, corrected by national courts to some degree, the legal template remains one-sided. This sows the seeds of trouble for the future. When law is ineffective, power relations tends to decide outcomes. For an example of a stiffer and more rigorous set of questions to determine whether delisting is justified, look at the seven-part test laid out by the press freedom group Article 19.[21]
11. There is a persistent and unjustifiable inequality between the 'interests' of some parties (such as search engines) and the rights of 'data subjects', which is wrong. The right to be forgotten lumps into one right people trying to correct and amend material they themselves have created (which should be uncontroversial) and a right to ask for the rectification of something published by a third party (which can be anything from an

internet troll to a respected news site), which should be the target of a more careful weighing of the rights of all those involved. The criteria for de-indexing or (in the future regulation) deletion are vague and subjective, derived from policies appropriate to an earlier information age. Opportunities have been missed to provide specific remedies for well-defined wrongs. To see a different legislative approach thought out from first principles, look at New Zealand's Harmful Digital Communications Act, passed in 2015.[22] This lists ten principles which outline what digital communications should not be, including threatening, offensive, menacing, a breach of confidence, a false allegation, or incitement to someone to send a harmful message. The Act continues to be debated, but it has the advantage of tackling specific harms in defined ways. Over-specific law will always run the risk of being overtaken by events or lacking the flexibility to cover the unforeseen. But the New Zealand law does appear to meet the test of proportional remedies for identifiable wrongs, thus minimising risks to free speech.

12. Compromise is required over the reach of EU law. At the time of writing, the French data protection authority is still requiring Google to de-index searches worldwide and not merely the European ones. They have fined the company €100,000 for failing to do this; Google have appealed the decision to France's highest civil court, the Conseil d'État and the case may well end up at the European Court. Before this stand-off Google had made it difficult (although not impossible) to use google.com from Europe; in March 2016, responding to an order from the UK ICO, the company applied geo-targeting techniques to spot and block users from Europe searching for delisted names. (An estimated 3 per cent of searches from Europe use a non-EU Google domain and searches on names would be a fraction of that total.) But this compromise has been rejected by France's CNIL, which insists on worldwide application. Google, supported by a coalition of American news organisations including Reuters, BuzzFeed, and News Corp,[23] argues that European data protection law should not determine what people outside the EU are allowed to see. They claim that making delisting work worldwide would be a cue for every repressive government in the world to try to do the same in a 'race to the bottom'. In theory, internet content about anything can be accessed from anywhere. But how wide is the interest in the past financial history of a man in Barcelona? The odds are that the interest will be strongest in Barcelona itself, a little less in the rest of Spain, and diminished by the time you reach Johannesburg or Jakarta.

Several commentators have suggested that a right to be forgotten might be graded by how local, national, or international interest might be and that de-indexing might be by the subtler means of determining delinking by geographic origin of the query and not by internet domain.[24]

Code, the market, and social conventions (aka norms) can all contribute to improving the balance between forgetting a little and being able to retrieve a lot. But whatever that contribution, solutions will have to be underpinned by law. The debate over how laws should be balanced should and will continue; this is not a closed question. To recall the importance of correcting and improving the right to be forgotten, we should remember why Google Spain came as such a surprise.

The decision alerted many people to legal powers they had not known existed. But it also clarified the extent of mission creep in data protection. The judgment in the case brought together in one document traditions and long-held assumptions of very varied kinds form all over Europe and illustrated the weaknesses of the intellectual genealogy of current law. Google Spain was not about defamation: that remains a separate, if cumbersome and expensive, area of law. Google Spain was not about the correction of inaccurate information: there was no dispute as to the accuracy of the original newspaper announcement. Google Spain was not about the wrongful release of private information: it was meant to be public. Google Spain was not about information doing harm. While Sr Costeja did claim that he had been distressed and embarrassed, the court made clear that this was not a requirement for getting a search engine to de-index something. The judgment took the risk to free speech and journalism into new territory.

Threats to free speech do not often occur as melodrama. Chilling effects work slowly and gently; their effects take time to be visible and their subtle nature makes them hard to measure. What has been delisted so far has only caused a small number of controversies and most parties have been content to accept Google's good intentions. The risk is a different one. The right to be forgotten, now built into the next iteration of EU law, symbolises procedures and practices which need to be reformed. That reform is needed because the right to be forgotten symbolises the failure to ensure that the balance between fairness to the individual and freedom of speech is as good as it can be.

Notes

Chapter 1   Law, Power, and the Hyperlink

1. http://curia.europa.eu/juris/document/document_print.jsf?doclang=EN&docid=152065 (accessed Mar. 2016).
2. Commission Nationale de l'Informatique et des Libertés.
3. See also Chapter 8.
4. George Brock, *Out of Print: Newspapers, Journalism and the Business of Journalism in the Digital Age* (Kogan Page, 2013).
5. Stefan Kulk and Frederik J. Zuiderveen Borgesius, 'Freedom of Expression and "Right to Be Forgotten" Cases in the Netherlands After Google Spain' (27 Aug. 2015), *European Data Protection Law Review*, 2015/2: 113–25. http://ssrn.com/abstract=2652171 citing Rechtbank Amsterdam, 13 Feb. 2015, ECLI:NL:RBAMS:2015:716 (accessed Apr. 2016).
6. Martin Moore, *Tech Giants and Civic Power* (Centre for the Study of Media, Communication & Power, King's College London, 2016), 4.
7. Cited in Moore, *Tech Giants*, 34.
8. http://www.emc.com/leadership/digital-universe/2014iview/executive-summary.htm. A zettabyte is one trillion gigabytes.
9. Natali Helberger et al., 'Regulating the New Information Intermediaries as Gatekeepers of Information Diversity', *Info*, 17/6 (Sept. 2015): 50–71.
10. Sergey Brin and Lawrence Page, 'The Anatomy of a Large-Scale Hypertext Web Search Engine', 1998. http://infolab.stanford.edu/~backrub/google.html (accessed Apr. 2016).
11. Email to author 22 Feb. 2016.
12. Jeffery Toobin, 'The Solace of Oblivion', *New Yorker*, 29 Sept. 2014.
13. *Japan Times*, 27 Feb. 2016. http://www.japantimes.co.jp/news/2016/02/27/national/crime-legal/japanese-court-recognizes-right-to-be-forgotten-in-suit-against-google/#.Vx0ys3Cf8fp (accessed Mar. 2016).
14. Email to author 18 Apr. 2016.
15. http://www.statista.com/topics/840/smartphones.
16. These were the figures for 2014.
17. Peter C. Evans and Annabelle Gawer, *The Rise of the Platform Enterprise: A Global Survey* (Centre for Global Enterprise, 2016).
18. The EU–US 'Safe Harbor' agreement of 2000, which provided for the transfer of data across the Atlantic, was ruled invalid by the European Court in October 2015.

19 Shoshana Zuboff, 'The Secrets of Surveillance Capitalism', *Frankfurter Allgemeine Zeitung*, 9 Mar. 2016. http://www.faz.net/aktuell/feuilleton/debatten/the-digitaldebate/shoshana-zuboff-secrets-of-surveillance-capitalism-14103616.html (accessed Apr. 2016).
20 Timothy Garton Ash, *Free Speech: Ten Principles for a Connected World* (Atlantic Books, 2016), 16.
21 Lucas D. Introna and Helen Nissenbaum, *Shaping the Web: Why the Politics of Search Engines Matter*, The Information Society 16 (2000), 16. https://www.nyu.edu/projects/nissenbaum/papers/ShapingTheWeb.pdf.
22 *The Times Magazine*, 18 Oct. 2014.
23 *Eurobarometer*, 359, 2011. http://ec.europa.eu/public_opinion/archives/ebs/ebs_359_en.pdf (accessed Feb. 2016).
24 *Daily Telegraph*, 11 Jan. 2010. http://www.telegraph.co.uk/technology/facebook/6966628/Facebooks-Mark-Zuckerberg-says-privacy-is-no-longer-a-social-norm.html (accessed Jan. 2016). See also: http://laboratorium.net/archive/2010/02/06/things_mark_zuckerberg_has_not_said (accessed July 2016).
25 Author interview, 8 Oct. 2015.
26 http://eur-lex.europa.eu/legal-content/EN/TXT/?uri=uriserv:OJ.L_.1995.281.01.0031.01.ENG (accessed Mar. 2016).
27 http://motherboard.vice.com/read/will-europes-right-to-be-forgotten-actually-hurt-the-web-we-asked-an-expert.
28 Formally known as the General Data Protection Regulation (GDPR). At the time of writing it seems improbable, given the UK referendum vote in June 2016 to leave the EU, that the GDPR will enter force in the UK. See Chapter 7.
29 See Chapter 2.
30 Agencia Española de Protección de Datos.
31 Google Spain, paragraph 17.
32 Mainly under the Digital Millennium Copyright Act in the US.
33 Author interview, 3 Nov. 2015.
34 https://www.google.com/transparencyreport/removals/europeprivacy/?hl=en (accessed Aug. 2016).
35 The UK Information Commissioner's Office had asked Google to reconsider 48 cases after one year.
36 S. Tippman and S. Pamiés, 'Google's Data on the Right To Be Forgotten', 2015. http://sytpp.github.io/rtbf/index.html (accessed July 2016).

Chapter 2   The Search Society

1 Adopted in 2000 and incorporated into the EU treaties in 2009.
2 Article 17. http://static.ow.ly/docs/Regulation_consolidated_text_EN_47uW.pdf (accessed Apr. 16).
3 Cass R. Sunstein in Levmore and Nussbaum, 106. Sunstein wrote as a Harvard professor; the essay was published while he served at the White House as head of the Office of Information and Regulatory Affairs.
4 Deputy Director, Commission de l'informatique et de libertés (CNIL). Author interview, 8 Oct. 2015.
5 Mark Coddington, *International Journal of Communication*, 6 (2012): 207–26.

6 Julia Powles, 'The Case That Won't Be Forgotten', *Loyola University Chicago Law Journal*, 47/2 (2015), 604.
7 http://www.thelavinagency.com/blog-big-data-speaker-douglas-merrill-talks-wall-street-and-credit-at-TEDx.html (accessed Feb. 2016).
8 Quoted by Ken Auletta, *Googled: The End of the World As We Know It* (Penguin, 2009), 138.
9 As part of the Human Rights Act 1998.
10 Daniel J. Solove, *Understanding Privacy* (Harvard University Press, 2008).
11 J. D. Lasica, cited by Alessia Ghezzi et al., *The Ethics of Memory in the Digital Age: Interrogating the Right to Be Forgotten* (Palgrave Macmillan. 2014), 11.
12 http://archive.wired.com/politics/law/news/1999/01/17538 26 Jan. 1999 (accessed Oct. 2016).
13 Natasha Lerner, *Index on Censorship*, 40/2 (2011), cited by Garton Ash, 287.
14 Henry H. Perritt, *Law and the Information Superhighway* (Aspen, 2001), 115.
15 Intelligence Squared debate, New York, 17 Mar. 2015. https://www.youtube.com/watch?v=yvDzW-2q1ZQ (accessed Mar. 2016).
16 Noberto Nunes Gomez de Andrade, in Ghezzi et al., *The Ethics of Memory*, 67.
17 James Q. Whitman, *The Two Western Cultures of Privacy: Dignity versus Liberty*. Yale University Law Faculty Scholarship Series, 649 (2004).
18 Seminar, Centre for European Legal Studies, Cambridge, Mar. 2015. http://www.cels.law.cam.ac.uk/activitiesactivities-archiveeu-internet-regulation-after-google-spain-dpnet15/session-recordings (accessed Mar. 2016).
19 Cited Aurelia Tamo and Damian George, 'Oblivion, Erasure and Forgetting in the Digital Age', *JIPITEC*, 5/2 (2014), Section III.1.
20 https://www.loc.gov/law/help/online-privacy-law/germany.php (accessed Feb. 2016).
21 ECHR *Wegrzynowski and Smolczewski v. Poland*. http://hudoc.echr.coe.int/eng?i=001-122365#{%22itemid%22:[%22001-122365%22]} The other landmark ECHR case is *Times Newspapers v. UK* 2009.
22 Privacy International, Data Protection http://www.privacyinternational.org/node/44 (accessed July 2016).
23 http://eur-lex.europa.eu/legal-content/EN/TXT/?uri=celex:32000L0031.
24 Manuel Castells, cited by Laidlaw, 'Private Power, Public Interest', 121.
25 Author interview, 8 Oct. 2015.
26 Statement on Internet Search Engines, AEPD, Madrid, 1 Dec. 2007.
27 Director of the AEPD to Constitutional Commission of Congress (Madrid), 28 Nov. 2007.
28 Frank Pasquale, *Reforming the Law of Reputation*, University of Maryland, Francis King Carey School of Law, Legal Studies Research Paper, 2016/3.
29 Viviane Reding, 30 Nov. 2010 http://europa.eu/rapid/press-release_SPEECH-10-700_en.htm (accessed Feb. 2016).

Chapter 3 Striking the Balance

1 https://qmro.qmul.ac.uk/.../FLANAGANDefiningJournalism2012PREPT (accessed Jan. 2016).
2 Matthew Ingram, *Fortune*, 9 May 2016. http://fortune.com/2016/05/09/facebook-media-principles (accessed May 2016).

3 David Erdos, *Confused? Analysing the Scope of Freedom of Speech Protection vis-à-vis European Data Protection*, Oxford Legal Research Paper 48 (2012), 9, n. 45.
4 Article 17.3 (a) and (b) of the GDPR. http://ec.europa.eu/justice/data-protection/reform/files/regulation_oj_en.pdf (accessed June 2016).
5 http://ec.europa.eu/justice/policies/privacy/docs/wpdocs/2009/wp163_en.pdf (accessed Feb. 2016).
6 Erdos, *Confused?*
7 Ibid.
8 See also Chapter 7.
9 Recital 18, GDPR.
10 Viviane Reding, Vice-President, European Commission, speech to European Data and Privacy conference, 30 Nov. 2010.
11 Article 29 Working Party press release, 18 June 2015.
12 David Leigh, quoted in Stephen Whittle and Glenda Cooper, *Privacy, Probity and the Public Interest* (Reuters Institute for the Study of Journalism, 2009), 23–4.
13 The General Data Protection Regulation, finalised 2016, due to enter force 2018. See Chapter 7.
14 See Chapter 5.

Chapter 4 Google Spain

1 www.etd.ceu.hu/2015/stupariu_ioana.pdf (accessed Jan. 2016).
2 http://curia.europa.eu/juris/document/document.jsf?docid=138782&doclang=EN.
3 Established in 1959 by the Council of Europe and thus distinct from – although often confused with – the European Court of Justice which oversees EU law.
4 Google Spain, paragraph 80.
5 Google Spain, paragraph 92.
6 European Commission official to the author, 3 Nov 2015.
7 ECHR *Wegrzynowski and Smolczewski* (see n. 21 ch. 2).
8 Kulk and Borgesius, 'Freedom of Expression'.
9 Google Spain, paragraphs 81 and 91.
10 Professor Peggy Valcke, interview on LSE media blog 4 Nov. 2014. http://blogs.lse.ac.uk/mediapolicyproject/2014/11/04/right-to-be-forgotten-tackling-the-grey-zones-and-striking-the-right-balance (accessed Feb. 2016).

Chapter 5 Reactions and Consequences

1 See later in this chapter.
2 TechCrunch: http://techcrunch.com/2014/06/07/wales-on-right-to-be-forgotten (accessed Feb. 2016).
3 https://inforrm.wordpress.com/2014/05/25/how-far-does-the-right-to-be-forgotten-extend-ashley-hurst (accessed Nov. 2015).
4 https://cpj.org/blog/2014/06/eu-right-to-be-forgotten-ruling-will-corrupt-histo.php (accessed Feb. 2016).

5 http://www.wired.co.uk/news/archive/2014-05/30/google-right-to-be-forgotten-form (accessed Jan. 2016).
6 https://www.facebook.com/VivianeRedingEU/posts/310790959087074 (accessed July 2016).
7 ICO seminar on the right to be forgotten, London, Nov. 2015 (quoted with permission).
8 The removal of URLs began on 26 June 2014.
9 Said by Google's chief privacy counsel to be a group numbering between 50 and 100 and largely based in Dublin.
10 Twitter and Reddit have made similar changes.
11 *Private Eye*, 1418 (13 May 2016).
12 https://www.google.com/advisorycouncil, report 6 Feb. 2015 (accessed Dec. 2015).
13 The latter when meeting as a group is known as the 'Article 29 Working Party'.
14 http://www.nytimes.com/2016/04/19/technology/google-europe-privacy-watchdog.html?ref=topics&_r=0 (accessed Jan. 2016).
15 https://www.google.com/transparencyreport/removals/europeprivacy/?hl=en (accessed May 2016).
16 http://www.theguardian.com/commentisfree/2014/jul/10/right-to-be-forgotten-european-ruling-google-debate (accessed Nov. 2015).
17 David Erdos, *European Regulatory Interpretation of the Interface between Data Protection and Journalistic Freedom: An Incomplete and Imperfect Balancing Act?* (29 Oct. 2015). University of Cambridge Faculty of Law Research Paper, 61/2015. Available at SSRN: http://ssrn.com/abstract=2683471 or http://dx.doi.org/10.2139/ ssrn.2683471.
18 http://www.husovec.eu/2014/05/should-we-centralize-right-to-be.html (accessed Jan. 2016).
19 http://www.theguardian.com/technology/2014/dec/01/microsoft-yahoo-right-to-be-forgotten (accessed Feb. 2016).
20 Article 29 Working Party, Guidelines on the implementation of Google Spain, adopted 26 Nov. 2014. http://www.dataprotection.ro/servlet/ViewDocument?id=1080 (accessed Apr. 2016).
21 See later in this chapter.
22 Article 29 Working Party, Guidelines.
23 *Financial Times*, 30 May 2014. https://next.ft.com/content/f3b127ea-e708-11e3-88be-00144feabdc0 (accessed Feb. 2016).
24 http://www.theguardian.com/technology/2015/jul/14/google-accidentally-reveals-right-to-be-forgotten-requests (accessed Jan. 2016).
25 See Chapter 1.
26 https://www.google.com/transparencyreport/removals/europeprivacy/faq/?hl=en (accessed Apr. 2016).
27 The author was one of 80 signatories.
28 https://infolawcentre.blogs.sas.ac.uk/2015/05/15/open-letter-to-google-from-80-internet-scholars-release-rtbf-compliance-data/.
29 Google Counsel William Malcolm, Seminar, Centre for European Legal Studies, Cambridge, Mar. 2015. http://www.cels.law.cam.ac.uk/activitiesactivities-archiveeu-internet-regulation-after-google-spain-dpnet15/session-recordings (accessed Mar. 2016).
30 Private information to author.

31 http://panopticonblog.com/2015/07/31/the-right-to-be-forgotten-and-the-county-court (accessed Feb. 2016).
32 Mark Scott, *New York Times*, 3 Oct. 2014. http://www.nytimes.com/2014/10/04/business/media/times-articles-removed-from-google-results-in-europe.html (accessed Mar. 2016).
33 http://www.bbc.co.uk/news/uk-wales-mid-wales-26820735.
34 http://www.bbc.co.uk/blogs/internet/entries/1d765aa8-600b-4f32-b110-d02fbf7fd379. The list covers the first year after the Google Spain judgment and lists 182 URLs removed (accessed Apr. 2016).
35 https://christopherstacey.wordpress.com/2015/11/11/the-google-effect-criminal-records-and-the-right-to-be-forgotten (accessed May 2016).
36 http://panopticonblog.com/2015/07/21/right-to-be-forgotten-claim-rejected-by-the-administrative-court (accessed Mar. 2016).
37 http://uitspraken.rechtspraak.nl/inziendocument?id=ECLI:NL:RBAMS:2014:6118 (accessed Feb. 2016). Summarised in English: https://inforrm.wordpress.com/2014/09/27/dutch-google-spain-ruling-more-freedom-of-speech-less-right-to-be-forgotten-for-criminals-joran-spauwen-and-jens-van-den-brink.
38 https://inforrm.wordpress.com/2015/06/10/third-dutch-google-spain-ruling-convicted-murderer-does-not-have-right-to-be-forgotten-emiel-jurjens (accessed Feb. 2016).
39 Keith Ross et al, *The Right to be Forgotten in the Media: A Data-Driven Study*, Proceedings on Privacy Enhancing Technologies 2016 (4), 1–14.
40 Accessed Feb. 2016.
41 Guidelines on the Implementation of the Court of Justice of the European Union judgment on *Google Spain and Inc v. AEPD and Mario Costeja Gonzalez*, C-131/12, 2, Nov. 2014.
42 ECHR, von Hannover v. Germany 2004. http://merlin.obs.coe.int/iris/2004/8/article2.en.html (accessed July 2016).
43 See Chapter 9.

Chapter 6 Beyond Europe

1 https://ec.europa.eu/digital-agenda/en/scoreboard/italy (accessed Feb. 2016).
2 http://www.camera.it/application/xmanager/projects/leg17/commissione_internet/testo_definitivo_inglese.pdf (accessed Feb. 2016).
3 https://inforrm.wordpress.com/2014/11/14/over-half-a-million-google-urls-removal-requests-to-date-the-right-to-be-forgotten-in-practice-sara-mansoori-and-eloise-le-santo/ (accessed Feb. 2016).
4 http://www.scmp.com/news/hong-kong/article/1533618/privacy-chief-allan-chiang-wants-right-be-forgotten-extended-asia (accessed Feb. 2016).
5 http://www.scmp.com/comment/insight-opinion/article/1534289/dont-follow-eus-bad-privacy-ruling-hong-kong (accessed Feb. 2016).
6 https://www.privacy.org.nz/blog/right-to-be-forgotten/ (accessed Feb. 2016).
7 Entities with a turnover above A$3m per annum.
8 https://www.oaic.gov.au/individuals/privacy-fact-sheets/general/privacy-fact-sheet-17-australian-privacy-principles (accessed Jan. 2016).

9 http://www.ft.com/cms/s/0/ade889d4-bc0e-11e4-a6d7-00144feab7de.html#axzz 40Fq9pOUI (accessed Feb. 2016).
10 http://www.japantimes.co.jp/news/2014/12/09/national/crime-legal/right-to-be-forgotten-on-the-internet-gains-traction-in-japan/#.V5eh5a5cNRk (accessed June 2016).
11 http://www.hldataprotection.com/2015/02/articles/international-eu-privacy/2015-the-turning-point-for-data-privacy-regulation-in-asia/(accessed Feb. 2016).
12 http://www.wsj.com/articles/google-wages-free-speech-fight-in-mexico-1432723483 (accessed Feb. 2016).
13 www.eliminalia.com (accessed Feb. 2016).
14 The American Declaration of the Rights and Duties of Man, the UN Universal Declaration of Human Rights, the American Convention on Human Rights, and the International Covenant on Civil and Political Rights.
15 Brazil, Colombia, Paraguay, Peru, Argentina, Ecuador, Panama, Honduras.
16 Argentina, Uruguay, Mexico, Peru, Costa Rica, Colombia.
17 Usually referred to in English as the Brazilian Civil Rights Framework for the Internet.
18 http://www.internetlab.org.br/wp-content/uploads/2015/10/Nota-t%C3%A9cnica_CTS-GPOPAI-ILAB.pdf#page=16 (accessed Jan. 2016).
19 https://www.eff.org/deeplinks/2015/10/brazils-terrible-pl215 (accessed Feb. 2016).
20 https://www.hse.ru/data/2015/10/11/1076267685/nurullaev.pdf.
21 http://in.rbth.com/politics/2015/07/15/new_right_to_be_forgotten_law_stirs_controversy_44235 (accessed Mar. 2016).
22 *Haynes v. Knopf*, cited by Solove, *Understanding Privacy*, 27.
23 Intelligence Squared debate, New York, 17 Mar. 2015. https://www.youtube.com/watch?v=yvDzW-2q1ZQ (accessed Mar. 2016).

Chapter 7   New Law: The General Data Protection Regulation

1 http://privacylawblog.fieldfisher.com/category/right-to-be-forgotten (accessed Mar. 2016).
2 Director of Intermediary Liability, Centre for Internet and Society, Stanford University, and previously Associate General Counsel at Google, dealing with right to be forgotten issues.
3 http://cyberlaw.stanford.edu/blog/2015/10/gdpr%E2%80%99s-notice-and-takedown-rules-bad-news-free-expression-not-beyond-repair#_ftnref7 (accessed Feb. 2016).
4 E.g. Finland, the Netherlands, and the UK: see Chapter 5.
5 David Erdos, *European Regulatory Interpretation of the Interface between Data Protection and Journalistic Freedom: An Incomplete and Imperfect Balancing Act?* (29 Oct. 2015). University of Cambridge Faculty of Law Research Paper, 61/2015.
6 Spain, the Czech Republic, and Croatia.
7 Such a facility is not a complete guarantee: there is risk of access to any copy which the network might archive and screen shots can be taken to preserve material.
8 Jack M. Balkin, 'Old School/New School Speech Regulation', *Harvard Law Review* 127 (2014), http://ssrn.com/abstract=2377526.
9 See n. 3 above.

10 The Information Commissioner's Office drew attention to this when responding to Google Spain.
11 http://britishlibrary.typepad.co.uk/webarchive/2014/07/a-right-to-be-remembered.html (accessed Mar. 2016).
12 http://www.ifla.org/node/10273 (accessed Mar. 2016).
13 https://www.manilaprinciples.org (accessed Mar. 2016).
14 EFF and Article 19 comment on GDPR. https://www.eff.org/files/2015/11/20/comment_on_gdpr_final.pdf (accessed Mar. 2016).
15 This example is theoretical: in reality, Sr Costeja's journey through the courts has left a large enough trail of information for his past life to be easily discoverable.
16 Powles, 'The Case That Won't Be Forgotten', 611.
17 Author interview, 2 Dec. 2015.

Chapter 8 Alternative Approaches

1 Accessed Feb. 2016.
2 The author has taken part in a project to design creative search for journalists, funded for a period by Google (see Acknowledgements section).
3 In the UK this is covered in the Contempt of Court Act 1981.
4 Mayer-Schönberger, *Delete*, 144–54.
5 https://vanish.cs.washington.edu.
6 http://www.digitaltrends.com/web/ways-to-decentralize-the-web/ and http://solid.mit.edu (accessed Aug. 2016).
7 http://www.theguardian.com/technology/2014/aug/21/islamic-state-isis-social-media-diaspora-twitter-clampdown (accessed Mar. 2016).
8 https://verdict.justia.com/2013/11/19/teens-online-eraser-laws (accessed Feb. 2016).
9 Zittrain, *The Future of the Internet*, 228–9.
10 http://www.theguardian.com/media/2016/feb/22/telegraph-suspends-comment-relaunched-online-content.
11 See Chapter 5.

Chapter 9 Conclusions: The Future

1 http://www.edelman.com/news/2016-edelman-trust-barometer-release/ (accessed Feb. 2016).
2 Eric Barendt, *Freedom of Speech* (2nd edn, Oxford University Press, 2007).
3 Jack Balkin, 'Old-School/New-School Speech Regulation', *Harvard Law Review*, 127 (2014), 2296.
4 Ibid.
5 See Chapter 1.
6 http://www.businessinsider.com/google-ceo-larry-page-wants-a-place-for-experiments-2013-5?IR=T (accessed July 2016).
7 http://www.businessinsider.com/google-ceo-larry-page-wants-a-place-for-experiments-2013-5?IR=T (accessed July 2016).
8 Accessed Mar. 2016.

9. http://georgebrock.net/andy-mitchell-and-facebooks-weird-state-of-denial-about-news.
10. https://globalfreedomofexpression.columbia.edu/wp/wp-content/uploads/2015/06/A-Callamard-Are-Courts-re-inventing-Internet-regulation-May-6-2015.pdf?37c4ff (accessed Jan. 2016).
11. Eugene Volokh and Donald Falk, *First Amendment Protection for Search Engine Results*. Google White Paper, 2012.
12. Video interview for Free Speech Debate. http://freespeechdebate.com/wp-content/uploads/2012/02/Wu-forgotten-subbed4.4.12.pdf (accessed Mar. 2016).
13. Pasquale, Frank, *Reforming the Law of Reputation*, University of Maryland, Francis King Carey School of Law, Legal Studies Research Paper, 2016/3.
14. Volokh and Falk, *First Amendment Protection*, 1–11.
15. *United States v. Stevens*, 130 S. Ct 1577, 1591 (2010), quoting *Cohen v. California*, 403 US 15, 25 (1971). Cited in Volokh and Falk, *First Amendment Protection*.
16. Erik Brynjolfsson and Andrew McAfee, *The Second Machine Age: Work, Progress and Prosperity in a Time of Brilliant Technologies* (Norton, 2014), 253.
17. http://www.careerbuilder.co.uk/share/aboutus/pressreleasesdetail.aspx?sd=6%2F26%2F2014&id=pr829&ed=12%2F31%2F2014 (accessed Feb. 2016).
18. See Chapter 5.
19. http://freespeechdebate.com/en/case/can-googles-algorithm-slander-a-politicians-wife (accessed May 2016).
20. See Chapter 7.
21. https://www.article19.org/data/files/medialibrary/38318/The_right_to_be_forgotten_A5-EHH-HYPERLINKS.pdf, pp. 21–6 (accessed Apr. 2016).
22. http://www.legislation.govt.nz/act/public/2015/0063/latest/whole.html (accessed Feb. 2016).
23. https://www.rcfp.org/sites/default/files/RCFP_CNIL_Sept14-English.pdf (accessed May 2016).
24. Brendan Alsenoy and Marieke Koekkoek, *The Extra-Territorial Reach of the EU's 'Right to Be Forgotten'* (19 Jan. 2015). ICRI Research Paper, 20.

Bibliography

Article 19, *The 'Right to Be Forgotten': Remembering Freedom of Expression* (Policy Brief, 2016). https://www.article19.org/resources.php/resource/38318/en/policy-brief:-the-right-to-be-forgotten.

Auletta, Ken, *Googled: The End of the World as We Know It* (Penguin, 2009).

Balkin, Jack, 'Old-School/New-School Speech Regulation', *Harvard Law Review*, 127 (2014), 2296.

Barendt, Eric, *Freedom of Speech* (2nd edn, Oxford University Press, 2007).

Brin, Sergey, and Page, Lawrence, 'The Anatomy of a Large-Scale Hypertext Web Search Engine', 1998. http://infolab.stanford.edu/~backrub/google.html (accessed Apr. 2016).

Brock, George, *Out of Print: Newspapers, Journalism and the Business of Journalism in the Digital Age* (Kogan Page, 2013).

Brynjolfsson, Erik, and McAfee, Andrew, *The Second Machine Age: Work, Progress, and Prosperity in a Time of Brilliant Technologies* (Norton, 2014).

Erdos, David, *Confused? Analysing the Scope of Freedom of Speech Protection vis-à-vis European Data Protection*, Oxford Legal Research Paper, 48 (2012). http://ssrn.com/abstract=2119187.

——, *European Regulatory Interpretation of the Interface between Data Protection and Journalistic Freedom: An Incomplete and Imperfect Balancing Act?* (29 Oct. 2015). University of Cambridge Faculty of Law Research Paper, 61/2015. Available at SSRN: http://ssrn.com/abstract=2683471 or http://dx.doi.org/10.2139/ssrn.2683471.

Evans, Peter C., and Gawer, Annabelle, *The Rise of the Platform Enterprise: A Global Survey* (Centre for Global Enterprise, 2016).

Garton Ash, Timothy, *Free Speech: Ten Principles for a Connected World* (Atlantic Books, 2016).

Ghezzi, Alessia, Guimarães Pereira, Ângela, and Vesnić-Alujević, Lucia, *The Ethics of Memory in the Digital Age: Interrogating the Right to be Forgotten* (Palgrave Macmillan, 2014).

Greenleaf, Graham, 'The Influence of European Data Privacy Standards Outside Europe: Implications for Globalisation of Convention 108' (19 Oct. 2011), *International Data Privacy Law*, 2/2 (2012); UNSW Law Research Paper, 2011/39; Edinburgh School of Law Research Paper, 2012/12. Available at SSRN: http://ssrn.com/abstract=1960299.

Helberger, Natali, Kleinen-von Königslöw, Katharina, and van der Noll, Rob, 'Regulating the New Information Intermediaries as Gatekeepers of Information Diversity', *Info*, 17/6 (Sept. 2015): 50–71.

Kulk, Stefan, and Borgesius, Frank Zuiderveen, 'Freedom of Expression and "Right to Be Forgotten" Cases in the Netherlands after Google Spain', *European Data Protection Law Review*, 2015/2. http://edpl.lexxion.eu/article/EDPL/2015/2/5.

Laidlaw, Emily B., 'Private Power, Public Interest: An Examination of Search Engine Accountability', *International Journal of Law and Information Technology*, 17/1 (2008), 113–45.

Levmore, Saul, and Nussbaum, Martha (eds), *The Offensive Internet: Speech, Privacy and Reputation* (Harvard University Press, 2012).

MacKinnon, Rebecca, *Consent of the Networked: The Worldwide Struggle for Internet Freedom* (Basic Books, 2013).

Mayer-Schönberger, Viktor, *Delete: The Virtue of Forgetting in the Digital Age.* Princeton University Press, 2009.

Moore, Martin, *Tech Giants and Civic Power*, Centre for the Study of Media, Communication & Power, King's College London, 2016.

Pasquale, Frank, *Reforming the Law of Reputation*, University of Maryland, Francis King Carey School of Law, Legal Studies Research Paper, 2016/3.

Perritt, Henry H., *Law and the Information Superhighway* (Aspen, 2001).

Powles, Julia, 'The Case That Won't Be Forgotten', *Loyola University Chicago Law Journal*, 47/2 (2015), 583–615. http://luc.edu/media/lucedu/law/students/publications/llj/pdfs/vol47/issue2/Powles.pdf.

Solove, Daniel J., *Understanding Privacy* (Harvard University Press, 2008).

Tamo, Aurelia, and George, Damian, 'Oblivion, Erasure and Forgetting in the Digital Age', *Journal of Intellectual Property, Information Technology and E-Commerce Law*, 5/2 (2014).

van Alsenoy, Brendan, and Koekkoek, Marieke, *The Extra-Territorial Reach of the EU's 'Right to Be Forgotten'* (19 Jan. 2015). ICRI Research Paper, 20. Available at SSRN: http://ssrn.com/abstract=2551838.

Volokh, Eugene, and Falk, Donald, *First Amendment Protection for Search Engine Results.* Google White Paper, 2012. http://ssrn.com/abstract=2055364.

Warren, Samuel, and Brandeis, Louis, 'The Right to Privacy', *Harvard Law Review*, 4/5 (Dec. 1890).

Whitman, James Q., The Two Western Cultures of Privacy: Dignity versus Liberty. Faculty Scholarship Series, 649 (2004). http://digitalcommons.law.yale.edu/fss_papers/649.

Whittle, Stephen, and Cooper, Glenda, *Privacy, Probity and the Public Interest.* Reuters Institute for the Study of Journalism, 2009.

Zittrain, Jonathan, *The Future of the Internet – and How to Stop it.* Yale University Press, 2008.

Zuboff, Shoshana, 'The Secrets of Surveillance Capitalism', *Frankfurter Allgemeine Zeitung*, 9 Mar. 2016. http://www.faz.net/aktuell/feuilleton/debatten/the-digital-debate/shoshana-zuboff-secrets-of-surveillance-capitalism-14103616.html.

Index

Administrative Court (England & Wales) 55
advertisements 19, 48, 92–3
Advocate-General opinions 1, 39–40
AEPD (Agencia Espanola de Proteccion de Datos) 12–13, 29, 38–9
algorithms of search engines 12, 18–20, 28–9, 82–5, 92, 98–9
Arapova, Galina 72
archives:
    libraries 79
    news 12–13, 25–7, 42, 44, 54
Argentina 68–70
Article 29 Working Party 50, 59, 61, 75
Australia 66–7
Austria 39
autocomplete functions 28–9, 98–9
automatic time expiry options 85

Baidu 93
balance of rights 31–3, 60, 75, 99
Balkin, Jack 78, 90
Ball, James 4–5
barriers to data retrieval 83–4
BBC (British Broadcasting Corporation) 15, 54, 55
Beggs, John 48
Belgium 23
Bernal, Paul 46–7
Bing 50, 98
Brandeis, Louis 20
Brazil 70–1
Brett Wilson LLP 59
Brin, Sergey 6
British Library 79
Brynjolfsson, Erik 96
BSG Resources Ltd 60

celebrities 48, 69
    see also public figures
censorship 46–7, 64, 72, 76, 78
Charter of Fundamental Rights (EU) 17, 42, 43
Chiang Yam-wang, Allan 64–5
Chile 70
chilling effects 17, 21, 23–4, 39, 66, 101
The Circle (Eggers) 28
civic powers of technology giants 4
CNIL (Commission de l'informatique et de libertés) 1, 3, 29, 32–3, 73–4, 100
collateral censorship 78
Colombia 70
Communications Commission (South Korea) 68
complaints processing by Google 15–16, 47, 48–54, 61
Constitutional Court (Germany) 7, 22–3, 27
content controls 96–7
Convention on Human Rights (EU) 17, 27, 72
convicted criminals:
    delisting by Google 52, 53, 54–7
    demotion of links 97
    EU approaches 6, 13, 14, 25–6
    non-EU approaches 7, 67, 70
copyright breaches 14, 47, 69, 85, 93
Costeja Gonzalez, Mario 12–13, 38, 41, 82, 91

INDEX

Council of Europe 22
Court of Human Rights (EU) 22, 27, 40, 42, 60
Court of Justice (EU):
   Google Spain case 1–2, 13–14, 36, 39–44, 71
   and journalism 32, 46
   criteria for delisting of data 39, 41, 43–4, 52–4, 100

Da Cunha, Virginia 69
Daily Mail 58
Daily Telegraph 58
data controllers 34, 39–41, 73–5, 77–8, 80, 99
Data Protection Act (UK) 58, 60, 73–4, 79
data protection authorities:
   and GDPR 79
   and Google complaints 35, 48–9, 56, 94, 97–8
   and Google Spain 3, 44
   guidelines for delisting 50, 59–62
   public knowledge of 10
   and search engines 38
   and social networking sites 33–4
   see also AEPD; CNIL; Garante; Information Commissioner's Office
Data Protection Directive (95/46/EC) 11, 35
data protection laws:
   development of 20–5, 27–8, 29–30, 99
   EU laws 11–13, 31–7
   and Google Spain 1–2, 42
   see also legislation
data quality principles 35
data subject rights 31, 41–2, 60, 61, 74–5, 99
de-indexing of data *see* delisting of data
decentralised networks 86
Declaration of Human Rights (UN) 17
Declaration of Internet Rights (Italy) 63–4
deletion of digital material:
   automatic options 85–6, 97
   danger of 36, 71

email messages 19
   personal data 10, 14, 66
   and the right to be forgotten 1, 35
   third-party content 77
delisting of data:
   cases in EU 41, 47–8, 54–8
   cases outside EU 7, 64, 66–7, 68–9
   criteria for 39, 41, 43–4, 52–4, 100
   danger of 36, 50–1
   Google complaints processing 15–16, 47, 48–54, 61
   guidelines for 50, 59–62
   search engine liability 38, 97
   self-regulation 29
demotion of links 97
Denmark 31
derecho al olvido 39
Diaspora 86
Digital Millennium Copyright Act (USA) 77
Digital Republic bill (France) 73–4
digital rights management (DRM) 85
Digitalis 84
Directive 95/46/EC (Data Protection) 11, 35
Directive 2000/31/EC (E-commerce) 28, 77, 79
diritto all'oblio 24
domestic abuse victims 14
droit à l'oubli 24
Drummond, David 49
Duffy, Janice 66–7

E-commerce Directive (2000/31/EC) 28, 77, 79
East Germany 12, 23
Edwards, John 65–6
Edwards, Malcolm 54
Electronic Frontier Foundation 71
Eliminalia 68
Erdos, David 32
European Charter of Fundamental Rights 17, 42, 43
European Commission 39, 47, 73
European Convention on Human Rights 17, 27, 72

114

INDEX

European Court of Human Rights 22, 27, 40, 42, 60
European Court of Justice:
  Google Spain case 1–2, 13–14, 36, 39–44, 71
  and journalism 32, 46
extra-territoriality 62

Facebook:
  algorithms of 19
  attitudes towards 9, 28
  content per minute 8
  delinking requests 51
  editorial responsibilities 90, 93
  news publishing 32
Federal Trade Commission (USA) 93
Finland 31, 56
First Amendment 7, 26, 72, 93–4
Fleischer, Peter 53
Floridi, Luciano 49
forget.me 59
forgetting 10–11, 12, 85
France:
  autocomplete functions 28–9
  awareness of data protection 10
  CNIL (Commission de l'informatique et de libertés) 1, 3, 29, 32–3, 73–4, 100
  convicted criminals 25
  data protection laws 12, 24
  delisted links 15, 54–5, 100
  Digital Republic bill 73–4
  privacy 22, 25, 26
  reputation management 59
  teacher-rating websites 32–3
France Télévisions 88
free speech:
  and criminal convictions 7
  and data protection 48, 76
  and delisting 39
  and journalism 4, 72
  in legislation 26, 31, 36–7
  in Mexico 68
  protection of 2, 10, 78–80, 99
freedom of expression:
  defences and justifications 90
  and Google Spain 40, 42–3, 94
  and harm 13
  in legislation 31–3, 66, 69, 71, 74–6
  and the right to be forgotten 7
  risks to 35
  and search engines 93
friction 83–4

GAFA corporations 8
Garante (Italian DPA) 38
General Data Protection Regulation (EU 2016/679) (GDPR) 11, 17, 33, 34, 73–81, 99
Germany:
  autocomplete functions 29
  Constitutional Court 7, 22–3, 27
  convicted criminals 6–7, 25–6, 52
  data protection laws 22, 23–4
  delisted links 15
  information control 12, 22–3
  newspaper archives 27
  teacher-rating websites 33
Girin, Bertrand 59
Global Witness 60
Google:
  algorithms of 2, 20, 82–3
  ambitions of 8
  autocomplete functions 28–9
  complaints processing 15–16, 47, 48–54, 61–2
  decision powers 98
  delisting of data 7, 41, 47–8, 54–8, 64, 66–7, 68–9
  editing of output 14, 93
  function of 28
  income of 19
  and the law 1–2, 3, 41, 91–5
  market shares 8, 91
  as publisher 66–7
  and reporting 90
  search histories 35
Google Spain case:
  description of 12–14, 38–44, 101
  impact of 1, 2–3, 14–15, 36, 58
  reactions and consequences 45–62
Graham, Christopher 81
guarantees of privacy 96

115

INDEX

Guardian 54, 58, 88
guidelines for delisting 50, 59–62

habeas data movement 70
Harmful Digital Communications Act (New Zealand) 100
Hegglin, Daniel 48
Hoboken, Joris van 11
Hong Kong 48, 64–5
honour, protection of 12–14, 25, 70
House of Lords (UK) 47
human rights:
    and access to information 40
    balance of 31–3
    codes of 17, 27, 66, 72
    Court of 22, 27, 40, 42, 60
    and Google Spain 41–2
Human Rights Act (UK) 17
Hungary 52
Hurst, Ashley 46

information capitalism 28
Information Commissioner's Office (UK) 10, 32, 52, 55, 60–1
information rights 89
informational self-determination 24–5
infrastructure of knowledge 14–16
International Federation of Library Associations (IFLA) 79
internet intermediaries 14, 76–81
Islamic State (IS) 86
Israel 64
Italy 15, 24, 26, 27, 38, 63–4

Jääskinen, Niilo 39–40
Japan 7, 67
Javid, Sajid 47
journalism:
    definition of 32
    exemptions for 26, 31–2, 39, 60–1
    online news 44, 87–8
    and the right to be forgotten 3–5
    risks to 89–91, 95–6

Kanda, Tomohiro 67
Kashaba, Mr 55

Keller, Daphne 75, 79
King, Geoff 46
KPMG partner delisting case 57
Kunis, Mila 48
Kutcher, Ashton 48

Lauber, Manfred 6
law firms and Google Spain 58–9
Law Reform Commission (Australia) 66
legislation:
    Charter of Fundamental Rights (EU) 17, 42, 43
    Data Protection Act (UK) 58, 60, 73–4, 79
    Data Protection Directive (95/46/EC) 11, 35
    Digital Millennium Copyright Act (USA) 77
    Digital Republic bill (France) 73–4
    E-commerce Directive (2000/31/EC) 28, 77, 79
    General Data Protection Regulation (EU 2016/679) 11, 17, 33, 34, 73–81, 99
    Harmful Digital Communications Act (New Zealand) 100
    Human Rights Act (UK) 17
    Marco Civil Da Internet 70–1
    PL215 71
    see also data protection laws
Leguizamon, Martin 69
Lessig, Lawrence 20, 96–7
libraries 6, 79
Lo, Alex 65

Mail Online 48
Malcolm, William 54
Manila Principles 80
Maradona, Diego 69
Marco Civil Da Internet 70–1
Mayer-Schönberger, Viktor 10–11, 85
McAfee, Andrew 96
McDonald, Dougie 57–8
McIntosh, Neil 55
McNamee, Joe 14
McNealy, Scott 22

memories in Europe 22–5
Merrill, Douglas 19
Mexico 68
Miyashita, Hiroshi 67
Mo, Claudia 65
Moran, Caitlin 9
Moran, Chris 58
Morvan, Yan 25
Mosley, Max 47–8
Moulin, Matthias 18, 29

Nazi use of information 22–3
Nemitz, Paul 24
Netherlands 15, 23, 56–7
New York Times 55
New Zealand 65–6, 100
news 4–5, 44, 87–8
  see also journalism
News of the World 47–8
newspapers 5–6, 25–7, 52, 60
  see also specific newspapers
Note2be.com 32–3
Nottingham Evening Post 54

obscurity of data 12, 65–6, 83
online intermediaries 14, 76–81
original publishers, rights of 44, 49, 51, 61, 98

Page, Larry 6, 91–2
El Pais 88
Le Parisien 54–5
Pasquale, Frank 95
personal and household activities 34
personal data 8, 34–5, 63–4, 70, 74–5
personal identity and reputation 24–5
Petit Mathieu 25
philosophies of data protection 25–30
photography and privacy 20
pictures 7–8, 25, 33–4, 47–8, 69, 85
Pink News 58
PL215 71
Poland 15, 25, 27, 34, 39, 42
Powles, Julia 18, 46
practical obscurity 12, 65–6, 83
Prism corporations 8

privacy:
  dimensions of 21–2, 23
  and free speech 2, 10
  and photography 20, 33–4
  public opinion of 9–10
  rights to 17, 25, 42–3
privacy laws:
  Asia-Pacific 66–8
  European 6–7, 21, 22, 26, 29, 74
  Latin America 68–71
  Russia 71–2
  USA 7, 20, 26, 72
Privacy Principle (Australia) 66
Private Eye 48
proportionality 40, 42–3, 63
protection of honour 12–14
public figures 36, 44
  see also celebrities
public interest:
  delisting of data 51–5, 59, 68
  disclosure of data 6, 32–3, 36, 71
  and GDPR 75–6
  and internet companies 42
  and journalism 95–6
  relevance of data 44
public opinion and privacy 9–10
publishers:
  Google 66–7
  rights of 44, 49, 51, 61, 98
purpose limitation 63, 80

Rallo Lombarte, Artemi 7, 13, 38
ratchet effect 36–7
rating websites 32–3
Reding, Viviane 34, 46
Regulation (EU) 2016/679 (General Data Protection) 11, 17, 33, 34, 73–81, 99
regulation of search engines 94–5
remembering 10–11
reputation 10–11, 24–5, 27, 59, 72, 84
reputational bankruptcy 86
Reputation.com 7
Rodriguez, Maria Belen 70

Russia 23, 25, 71–2
Rwanda 23

Safe Harbor doctrine 8
scope and language 33–6
search engines:
   and advertising 19, 92–3
   algorithms 12, 18–20, 28–9, 82–5, 92, 98–9
   and freedom of expression 90, 93
   and GDPR 76–81
   Google Spain case 38–42
   market shares 91
   regulation of 94–5
   smaller 50
   and social responsibility 94, 97
   trust of 89
Sedlmayr, Walter 6–7
self-regulation system 29
Sipple, Oliver 26
Snowden, Edward 40
social media 11, 34, 51
social networks:
   data changes 29, 86
   expiry of data 97
   and laws 33–5
   and news 4, 6, 87
   and privacy issues 21
   transparency of 94
South Korea 67–8
Spain *see* Google Spain case
spickmich.de 33
Streisand effect 58–9
Sunstein, Cass 17
Supreme Court (USA) 96
surveillance 5, 8, 40, 70, 78, 90
Sweden 15, 23, 26, 31–2

takedown clauses 76–7
teacher-rating websites 32–3
De Telegraaf 57
Tench, Dan 58–9
time expiry options 85
transparency of decisions 51, 81, 94, 98

uncontrolled documents 6–10
United Kingdom:
   convicted criminals 25
   Data Protection Act (UK) 58, 60, 73–4, 79
   data protection awareness 10
   delisted links 15, 48, 52, 55, 58, 79
   Facebook, attitudes to 9
   Human Rights Act 17
   journalism, views on 60–1
   privacy laws 21
   publishing restrictions 14
   response to Google Spain 47
United Nations Declaration of Human Rights 17
United States of America:
   delisted links 55
   Digital Millennium Copyright Act 77
   First Amendment 7, 72
   privacy issues 23
   privacy laws 7, 20, 26
   reset of digital life 86, 94
Unvanish project 86

La Vanguardia 12–13, 38
Vanish project 85–6

Wales, Jimmy 45
Warren, Samuel 20
webmasters 51, 61
   see also publishers
Werlé, Wolfgang 6–7
Wikimedia Foundation 7
Wikipedia 6–7
Wu, Tim 94–5

Yahoo 50, 67, 69, 98
Yamada, Kenta 67
Yandex 72
YouTube 8

Zittrain, Jonathan 72, 86
Zuboff, Shoshana 8
Zuckerberg, Mark 10

RISJ/I.B.TAURIS PUBLICATIONS

CHALLENGES

The Right to be Forgotten: Privacy and the Media in the Digital Age
George Brock
ISBN: 978 1 78453 592 6

The Kidnapping of Journalists: Reporting from High-Risk Conflict Zones
Robert G. Picard and Hannah Storm
ISBN: 978 1 78453 589 6

Innovators in Digital News
Lucy Küng
ISBN: 978 1 78453 416 5

Journalism and PR: News Media and Public Relations in the Digital Age
John Lloyd and Laura Toogood
ISBN: 978 1 78453 062 4

Reporting the EU: News, Media and the European Institutions
John Lloyd and Cristina Marconi
ISBN: 978 1 78453 065 5

Women and Journalism
Suzanne Franks
ISBN: 978 1 78076 585 3

Climate Change in the Media: Reporting Risk and Uncertainty
James Painter
ISBN: 978 1 78076 588 4

Transformations in Egyptian Journalism
Naomi Sakr
ISBN: 978 1 78076 589 1

BOOKS

Journalism and the NSA Revelations: Privacy, Security and the Press
Risto Kunelius, Heikki Heikkilä, Adrienne Russell and
Dmitry Yagodin (eds)
ISBN: 978 1 78453 675 6 (HB); 978 1 78453 676 3 (PB)

Journalism in an Age of Terror: Covering and Uncovering the Secret State
John Lloyd
ISBN: 978 1 78453 708 1

Media, Revolution and Politics in Egypt: The Story of an Uprising
Abdalla F. Hassan
ISBN: 978 1 78453 217 8 (HB); 978 1 78453 218 5 (PB)

The Euro Crisis in the Media: Journalistic Coverage of Economic Crisis and European Institutions
Robert G. Picard (ed.)
ISBN: 978 1 78453 059 4 (HB); 978 1 78453 060 0 (PB)

Local Journalism: The Decline of Newspapers and the Rise of Digital Media
Rasmus Kleis Nielsen (ed.)
ISBN: 978 1 78453 320 5 (HB); 978 1 78453 321 2 (PB)

The Ethics of Journalism: Individual, Institutional and Cultural Influences
Wendy N. Wyatt (ed.)
ISBN: 978 1 78076 673 7 (HB); 978 1 78076 674 4 (PB)

Political Journalism in Transition: Western Europe in a Comparative Perspective
Raymond Kuhn and Rasmus Kleis Nielsen (eds)
ISBN: 978 1 78076 677 5 (HB); 978 1 78076 678 2 (PB)

Transparency in Politics and the Media: Accountability and Open Government
Nigel Bowles, James T. Hamilton and David A. L. Levy (eds)
ISBN: 978 1 78076 675 1 (HB); 978 1 78076 676 8 (PB)

Media and Public Shaming: Drawing the Boundaries of Disclosure
Julian Petley (ed.)
ISBN: 978 1 78076 586 0 (HB); 978 1 78076 587 7 (PB)